HONDA

HONDA

An American Success Story

Robert L. Shook

PRENTICE HALL PRESS

NEW YORK LONDON TORONTO SYDNEY TOKYO

*This book
is dedicated to
Carrie, RJ, and Michael*

Prentice Hall Press

Gulf+Western Building
One Gulf+Western Plaza
New York, New York 10023

Library of Congress Cataloging-in-Publication Data

Shook, Robert L.
  Honda: An American Success Story

  Bibliography: p.
  Includes index.
    1. Honda of America Mfg. 2. Automobile industry
and trade—United States. 3. Automobile industry and
trade—Japan. 4. Motorcycle industry—United States.
5. Motorcycle industry—Japan. I. Title.
HD9710.U54H667   1988   338.7'6292'0973   88-12497
ISBN 0-13-394610-X

Manufactured in the United States of America

10 9 8 7 6 5 4 3 2 1

First Edition

Acknowledgments

About ten years ago, I set a lifetime goal to write twenty books. And at age forty-eight, upon achieving that goal, I raised my quota to an additional twenty. After completing *The IBM Way* in 1986 with Buck Rodgers, I wanted to do a book about a comparable company with the same brand of excellence. This was no easy task. What does one do for an encore after IBM?

I chose to write *Honda: An American Success Story*. After researching many multinational corporations, I concluded that Honda is indeed the most intriguing and innovative company of the 1980s. After reading this book I believe many others will share my opinion.

It would not have been possible to write this book without the cooperation of the company's management. The preparation of the manuscript required interviews with hundreds of people within the Honda organization throughout the United States and Japan. It took both confidence and conviction on management's part to permit an independent author to write this book—confidence in knowing that I would portray the company as it really is; and conviction in its corporate philosophy, allowing me to share it with those interested in learning an innovative management style. I want to thank Honda's management for its faith and understanding.

I thank all of the individuals at Honda and at other organizations who volunteered to sit through my extensive interviews; many lasted for several hours. In fact, I speculate that the accumulative hours totaled an amount equaling the production time required to manufacture a sizable fleet of cars! I want to apologize in advance to anyone whose name I inadvertently fail to acknowledge. Please observe that the following people are listed alphabetically: John Adams, John Aler, Charles Allen, Greg Ament, John Andrews, Toshi Amino, Brian Baker, Glenn Barr, Gerry Bengtson, Erik Berkman, Jack Billmyer, Jan Blanton, Kevin Brletic, Joan Burns, Tetsuo Chino, John Christman, Lin Clements, Robert Cole, Susie Comer, Gary Crawford, J. R. Cunningham, David Dalby, Marion Donahoe, James Duerk, E. J. Edminister, Tom Elliott, Don English, Stu Everett, Masahiro Fujiwara, Tim Gansheimer, Tim Garrett, Denise Garrison, Mary Beth Hamilton, Bill Hayes, Rick Hemp, Sadie Hodge, John Hofmann, Bob Hrivnak, Wendy Iden, Kiyoshi Ikemi, Len Immke, Susan Insley, Shoichiro Irimajiri, Yoshi Ishida, Makoto Itabashi, Larry Jenkins, Larry Jermyn, Kaname Kasai, Kihachiro Kawashima, David King, Al Kinzer, Fumito Kobayashi, Osamu Kobayashi, Ted Kondo, Mike Kreglow, Tadashi Kume, Shelley Lanza, Dennis Lee, Bert Lindsay, Lou Martin, Bob Mateo, Kiyoshi Miyaki, Takeomi Miyoshi, Elmo Mossbarger, Bob Muth, Brian Newman, Leon Nicol, Moto Nishimura, April O'Dale, Shin Ohkubo, Satoshi Okubo, Ritsuko Onodera, Susan Osborn, Hiroshi Oshima, John Petas, John Pleiman, Chris Poland, Steve Powell, Kelly Quinn, Dennis Reese, Steve Reissig, Jewel Ray, Ralph Ricketts, Gerry Rubin, L. Jack Ruscilli, Perry Rutan, Karen Sabo, Cliff Schmillen, Al Seitter, Cedrick Shimo, Darrell Shown, Bob Simcox, Dan Smith, Polly Smith, Pat Sparks, Tadao Sugiura, Barnie Sullivan, Shin Tanaka, Bill Taylor, Colleen Teets, Willie Tokishi, Rich Tsukamoto, Mary Wallace, Mike Wallace, Scott Whitlock, Joe Williams, Ray Wilt, Jim Wolever, James Womack, Steve Yoder, Shige Yoshida, and Koichiro Yoshizawa.

I also say thank you (*arigato gozaimasu*) to my three charming interpreters, Hiroko Kayo, Yumiko Ishiguro, and Yuko Ito, who assisted me in Japan with interviews that would not have otherwise been possible. And my deep appreciation to my secretary, Mary Liff, who had the difficult task of transcribing recorded interviews that totaled more than 2,000 legal-size pages! As usual, Mary also did a superb job typing and assisting me with the extensive organizational work required to prepare the manuscript. And Susan Prentice's assistance in preparing my second draft of the manuscript was outstanding.

I am grateful to Shogo Iizuka, Kurt Antonius, and Roger Lambert, my first contacts with Honda, who continued to work with me throughout the entire preparation of the manuscript. And I am deeply indebted to Jeff Leestma who served as my liaison. Jeff was also an excellent source, directing me to where and from whom I could get the necessary information I sought to write this book. His cooperation was invaluable.

My gratitude to my good friend and agent, Al Zuckerman, who provided me with considerable encouragement and feedback throughout the writing of this book. And it was a pleasure to have the opportunity to work with my editor, Paul Aron, a fine person and a true professional.

The writing of this book was truly a team effort. We did it the Honda Way!

Contents

II *A Customer-driven Company*

4 *The American Marketing Organization*   57

5 *Providing Superior Service*   76

III *Building with People*

6 *Respect for the Individual*   89

7 *The Teamwork Factor*   101

Contents · xi

IV   *A Corporate Philosophy*

Contents · xiii

Introduction

Early in the 1980s, while U.S. industry was searching for excellence, along came Honda. In late 1982, just three years after the company started manufacturing motorcycles in the United States, Honda became the first Japanese company to manufacture automobiles on American soil.

When the auto plant officially opened its doors in Marysville, Ohio, the world's leading motorcycle manufacturer was well on its way to becoming recognized as a front-runner in the automobile industry, which was quite a feat for a company that didn't produce a single car until the early 1960s.

By the time the plant debuted, Honda motorcycles and automobiles had become accepted products in America. During this same period, the quality of U.S. automobiles was deteriorating at an alarming rate and consumers expressed their concern about buying an American-made Honda. The message voiced across much of the nation was: "U.S. labor isn't capable of making cars of the same quality as the Japanese." Many said they would buy only those Hondas made in Japan. Even dealers complained that the anticipated inferior quality of workmanship at the new plant would ruin their businesses.

In spite of these protests, the new plant went into production using a labor pool from small, rural communities in central Ohio. Most of the workers had farming backgrounds; only a few had worked in manufacturing. When the first Accords rolled off the assembly line, industry analysts eagerly gathered to inspect these early models. The overwhelming consensus was that the Ohio-produced automobiles had, indeed, equaled the quality of those cars produced in Japan. Today the quality workmanship of Honda's American-made cars is widely accepted as the epitome of excellence.

The Honda of America Manufacturing, Inc. (HAM) plant has become a showcase for all U.S. manufacturing companies, and today testifies that American workers are fully capable of producing outstanding workmanship. To the surprise of many who have visited the HAM plant, the levels of automation and technology are not so different from what exists at other modern automotive factories. It is not the machines but the people who make the difference in quality and productivity. The plant's performance serves as a reminder that America's work force does have the ability to excel in a world marketplace.

American industrialists are often quick to attribute others' success, especially that of Japanese companies, to "unfair" government intervention, or unfair labor practices. Yet it was Honda's *managerial* innovations that transformed a group of central Ohio people into a highly motivated and inspired work force. These innovations result in a corporate behavior that marches to the beat of a different drummer. This unwritten management style is sometimes known as the Honda Way—a philosophy responsible for a corporate culture that strongly influences the daily and long-term activities of the company. It is the Honda Way that has created a working environment in which people take pride in their jobs. There are no adversarial us-them relationships between management and labor. Instead, there is an atmosphere in which people become involved in their work, and teamwork thrives. People care about the welfare of the company because they know the company cares about them.

Honda's achievement is truly an American success story, a story of how quality products can be made and sold by Americans in America. The message is clear: The U.S. work force can compete favorably in a world marketplace. However, management styles and attitudes must be changed if the United States is to enter the twenty-first century as a major world economic leader. If change is resisted, it must resign itself to being a second-rate industrial nation.

Honda: An American Success Story is not a theoretical treatise but the true story of how one company operates its business exceedingly well. And it tells explicitly how this success can be emulated by managers in all fields. What American industry must do to recapture its competitive edge cannot be legislated, nor can it be done overnight. It requires long-term planning. American management must devise methods to produce quality products and simultaneously provide exceptional service. The good news is that it is not too late—what Honda does so well can be implemented throughout American industry.

Honda was a unique organization, a maverick, from the start. Soichiro Honda founded the company in 1948 with an investment of only $3,200 by buying surplus engines and attaching them to bicycles to provide cheap transportation. From this humble beginning, the eighth-grade dropout and son of a blacksmith built the world's largest motorcycle company within twelve years. This was an amazing feat under any circumstances, especially in a country where almost 250 other companies also were engaged in the motorcycle business.

In its early years, the company had to struggle to survive, and frequently engaged in bitter, painful battles against the establishment—the Japanese government as well as the centuries-old, giant trading companies that dictated Japanese business policy and convention. Honda had to undertake another uphill battle when it first began marketing products in the United States in 1959. And Honda again met with resistance in 1982, when it became the first Japanese company to build automobiles in the United States.

Those early struggles, along with many other obstacles Honda overcame, are described in part I of this book. Parts II and III give a full account of the unique management style of Honda, an organization recognized today as a dynamic, risk-taking company, one known for its innovation and its un-Japanese ways. Finally, part IV is a summary of this remarkable company's philosophy.

From the beginning, skeptics in the United States and Japan refused to believe that Honda, a Johnny-come-lately, could survive in the mature and capital-intensive automobile industry. Due to its late start, Honda had to play catch-up. In doing so it developed an aggressive attitude that resulted in a management style predicated on becoming a *different company*. Even today, this giant multinational corporation is viewed in Japan as a nonconforming organization, one that dares to defy the bedrock traditions of its Japanese culture.

At present, Honda Motor Company, with estimated revenues of $24 billion, is the largest Japanese company started since World War II. Today, Honda produces cars, motorcycles, and power equipment in sixty-six plants in thirty-five countries in Asia, Europe, South America, and North America, and enjoys a reputation for turning out excellent products at reasonable prices. Its motorcycles and cars are praised for their design and technological superiority, and Honda dealers are acclaimed for providing outstanding service.

Honda: An American Success Story goes far beyond the Japanese management practices discussed in other books. This is a story about a hybrid company, one that is part Japanese, part American; part of each country in which it does business. In particular, this book spotlights the company's manufacturing and marketing practices in the United States, and how, after only twenty-five years in the automobile industry, it has become America's fourth largest seller and manufacturer of cars.

Honda enjoys an outstanding reputation for its technological excellence. But the lion's share of the company's success must be credited to a prodigiously productive work force that consistently builds and markets high-quality products. Above all, this book is a study of how Honda management works with people. In general, similar technologies are shared by every major company within the automobile industry. Rarely can a technological breakthrough push one auto maker above the others for the long term. So, making the best use of human resources is where the *real* Honda difference lies. The management principles discussed in this book start from this message, and both the message and the techniques transcend national boundaries.

I

The Honda Story

1

The Honda Motor Company: The Beginning

IN 1946, a broken Japan was struggling to rebuild from the rubble and debris of war. Barely a year had passed since the last bombs had fallen, and much had been done to shore up the remains and purge the dreadful reminders. Still, much of the city remained in ruins. What little transportation Tokyo had available consisted of smoking, motorized vehicles fed through charcoal-burning converters or garrulous streetcars that threatened to expire on the spot should one more passenger try to board. And then there were the bicycles.

Bicycles were not only plentiful but suitable for transporting both rider and cargo at seemingly rapid speeds. Yet no matter how determined the cyclist might be, he or she couldn't carry very much or go very far.

That year, forty-year-old Soichiro Honda founded the Honda Technical Research Institute. Here, small internal combustion engines and machine tools were developed to produce motorized bicycles. The scenario could not have been more adverse. Honda was undercapitalized and about to enter an overcrowded industry that already had roughly 250 competitors. Honda was a man with little formal education and he possessed no managerial or business skills. If there had been business planners and consultants by his side, he would have been strongly advised to abort his new venture and salvage whatever capital he had left.

SOICHIRO HONDA: THE MAN WHO LOVED MACHINES

Soichiro Honda was the son of a poor blacksmith in the small village of Komyo, about 270 kilometers southwest of Tokyo. As a sideline, his father repaired bicycles. The young boy grew up with the pounding sounds of the anvil, and perhaps it was this background that instilled in him a lifelong love for machines. Even before he started school, Soichiro Honda helped his father repair bicycles.

When he answered a small help-wanted ad in one of his father's trade magazines, his formal education abruptly ended. At age sixteen, Honda headed to Tokyo to serve a six-year apprenticeship with Art Shokai, a small automobile repair shop. It was a humble beginning in the automotive field, with his first month's pay totaling $1.25. Yet when the six-year period ended, the twenty-two-year-old man had developed excellent skills as a repairman. His employer put up the money that allowed Honda to open his own branch of the Art Shokai in his hometown.

It was a labor of love. Honda worked long, hard hours and the business was a modest success. In his spare time, he tinkered with engines. In what seemed to be a natural sequence of events, he became fascinated with fast cars and eventually began to design and build them so he could enter racing events. In July 1936, Honda entered the All-Japan Speed Rally in which he drove a modified Ford. Traveling at a speed of around 75 miles per hour (120 km per hour), he set a new Japanese average speed record. He held a comfortable lead coming into the home stretch, when suddenly a disabled car crashed violently into his, leaving him badly injured and incapacitated for eighteen months. His wife, Sachi, a local farmer's daughter, was able to persuade him to quit race car driving. This was a turning point in the mechanic's life—it forced him to forsake his ambition to pursue a racing career, and he devoted his time and energy to his business.

But Honda eventually began to grow restless with his auto repair business.

Repairing cars is limited, he reasoned, because I can repair cars for people only in the local and surrounding areas. People from America, or even Tokyo, are not going to bring their cars to my shop, no matter how well I repair them. But if I were in the manufacturing end of the business, I could expand into markets in faraway places.

In late 1937, with some financial backing from relatives and friends, Honda bought some machinery to start a piston ring factory. His determination to succeed was so intense that he literally lived at his factory, sleeping on the floor. He refused to take time to leave the shop, so his wife brought in meals. Still the business floundered. One day a friend who owned a foundry advised, "No matter how hard you labor and want to succeed, you must become an expert at casting or you are doomed to fail. I recommend you serve an apprenticeship to learn the business."

Recognizing his limitations and his need for more knowledge, Honda consulted a professor at the nearby Hamamatsu School of Technology (now Shizuoka University) and was told his piston rings did not use enough silicone. He recalls, "Not only did I not have enough knowledge about silicone, but I was ashamed to admit that I didn't even know I needed it."

A poor student during his school days, Honda reluctantly attended classes while continuing to run his business. Honda stubbornly paid little attention to anything in class that did not relate directly to piston rings. He took no notes, nor did he bother to take written examinations. The head of the school told him he would not receive a diploma if he refused to be tested. With that, Honda retorted that a diploma had less value than a movie ticket. "A ticket will get you a seat in a movie theater, but a diploma won't get you a job!"

It was not that Honda did not respect other people's education: He simply was not impressed with book knowledge that was not backed by experience. For years, he had a strong contempt for the Japanese *gakubatsu,* the "good old boy" networking system that placed more emphasis on what school a person graduated from than on his or her ability to perform on the job.

Even now, a degree from a major university can open otherwise closed doors within the Japanese business community. While Honda Motor Company has its share of college graduates, a diploma from the "right" school has no bearing on landing a job in the company.

Once Honda learned the proper way to build piston rings, his company grew, and within two years it landed a significant contract with Toyota, Japan's largest auto maker. During World War II, fire bombings severely damaged his piston factory, and as the war ended an earthquake destroyed what remained of the business.

In October 1946, Honda established the Honda Technical Research Institute, a tiny firm with a fancy name. It was composed of its founder and a handful of associates. For two years Honda tinkered with engines. Then, in 1948, he reorganized his company and renamed it Honda Motor Company Ltd. For about $3,200, he bought 500 small war surplus engines. These were small gasoline engines that had been used as electrical generators during the war, the tiny two-stroke, single-cylinder kind that could be adapted to provide auxiliary power for bicycles.

Like many commodities in Japan, gasoline was scarce and expensive. So Soichiro Honda began to make his own special, cheap concoction of turpentine oil and gasoline. Predictably, his customers began to buy fuel from the fledgling company, which led to a modest amount of repeat business. The first year, total sales grossed $55,000 with no profits. When the supply of surplus motors began to run out, the hard-driving inventor decided that he should build his own engines.

A PARTNERSHIP MADE IN HEAVEN: ENTER TAKEO FUJISAWA

While the demand for his engines was high, Honda had virtually no marketing experience; his personal interests were focused on the mechanical end of his business. Realizing that his products had to be sold, he entered an agreement with a distributor who purchased all of the rebuilt engines and, in turn, packaged them to sell as motorcycle conversion kits for bicycles. Relieved of the marketing burden, Honda was able to continue tinkering with engines in his constant pursuit to develop a "better mousetrap." He firmly believed that if Japan were to be built into a major industrial nation, the nation's salvation would come through advanced technology.

In 1949, Honda raised $3,800 from outside investors and put the money toward developing lightweight, 50-cubic-centimeter, two-cycle engines capable of generating 3 horsepower. Its higher horsepower not only was more reliable than the competition's but the motorcycle had a stamped metal frame that was superior. During a company celebration party, somebody described the new product as "a dream." With that remark, it officially was christened: "Dream Type D." With the new model's success, the company enjoyed a brief spurt of prosperity. Honda's small factory increased its work force to seventy employees and its monthly production rate climbed to 100 units by the end of 1949.

Sales could have been even higher if Honda's exclusive distributor had not made the decision to artificially limit monthly sales to 80 units. By keeping the supply lower than the demand, the distributor was able to enjoy a higher margin, but it certainly was not in the best interest of Honda. Progress came to an abrupt halt when the competition leapfrogged Honda's two-cycle model with a quieter and more powerful four-stroke engine. The struggling enterprise was faced with the double dilemma of manufacturing an obsolete product and dealing with a self-serving distributor. Honda was desperately in need of managerial expertise. That expertise came in the form of Takeo Fujisawa.

Four years Honda's junior, Takeo Fujisawa was the son of a small entrepreneur. Like Soichiro Honda, Fujisawa discontinued his formal education at an early age, having finished only middle school. The depression and his father's illness had forced Fujisawa to leave school to support his family. In 1929, he took a job addressing envelopes and postcards for pennies a day. After one year of addressing letters, he joined the Imperial Army as a volunteer cadet. As a volunteer he was able to quit after serving only one year. Not qualified for a better position, Fujisawa again began addressing letters, and continued at this until 1934 when he was hired as a sales clerk for Mitsuwa Shokai, a small steel merchant in Tokyo. His starting monthly income was 15 yen, about one-third of his former salary, but by the end of his second year he became the company's top salesman, earning 150 yen a month.

In July 1937, Japan invaded China, marking the beginning of the Sino-Japanese War. When the owner of Mitsuwa Shokai entered the military service, the twenty-seven-year-old Fujisawa was put in charge of the business. The war created a big demand for steel, and under Fujisawa's guidance the company's profits grew. In 1939, just before the beginning of World War II, Fujisawa established the Japan Machine and Tool Research Institute, a company that made its profits by manufacturing, cutting, and grinding tools for the Sino-Japanese War effort. With bonuses that his boss paid him after returning from the war, Fujisawa became a man of modest means.

During World War II, while Soichiro Honda was in the piston ring business, he met Hiroshi Takeshima, a buyer for the Nakajima Aircraft Company. In a twist of fate, during the summer of 1948, while visiting the Yasukuni Shrine in Tokyo, Takeshima bumped into an old friend, Fujisawa. Sometime during their conversation, Fujisawa mentioned that he was looking for a business in which to invest some of his money. Takeshima recommended Honda.

It wasn't until August 1949 that Fujisawa met Honda at Takeshima's home. "All of the local investors in Hamamatsu want a quick return on their money," Honda told his new acquaintance, "and to develop the proper technology to make competitive engines, I need investors who are willing to make a long-term commitment."

It took only a brief conversation for the two men to agree to work together. On a handshake, Fujisawa made a commitment to invest $7,500 of his own money and to raise additional financing to provide Honda with the funds to build engines. It was decided that each would concentrate on his own area of expertise: Honda would devote his energy to technology, and Fujisawa would be in charge of financing and marketing.

In describing the two men's working relationship, Honda said:

> Assuming that reaching the top of Mount Fuji was the ultimate goal, both Fujisawa and I had the same goal. But I took one route, while he took another because he had a different philosophy and personality. If we had been taking the same route, we both might have been finished off by an unexpected storm. Instead we were able to communicate with each other because we were taking different routes. Fujisawa would say to me, "I am at such and such a place, and I see a storm coming. So be careful!" Then I would be careful. We had heart-to-heart communication, although we were at different places and acted differently. Yet, we had the same goal of reaching the top of that mountain.

In March 1950, Fujisawa was named the director of sales and opened an office in Tokyo. By September Honda had moved from Hamamatsu to Tokyo, which had become Japan's center of financing and manufacturing, replacing Osaka as the commercial capital. Honda believed that the nation's capital was the place to be.

Once headquarters was in Tokyo, Honda heeded the advice of his new partner that he should quit tinkering with his noisy, two-stroke engine and concentrate on building a better four-stroke model or, as Fujisawa put it, "Be prepared to face extinction." Fujisawa believed that the company's existing engines made unpleasant, high-pitched noises. As a result, he could sign up only mediocre distributors who carried Honda's products as a secondary line. By 1951, Honda had succeeded in introducing a breakthrough design for a new four-stroke engine with double the competition's horsepower. Demand for the new engine was solid, and by 1952, Fujisawa was able to raise $88,000 to invest in manufacturing and increased marketing efforts.

Monthly production again zoomed, and Honda landed a contract to sell its entire engine inventory to a company called Kitagawa. Kitagawa attached the Honda products to its own motorcycle bodies and resold them to distributors throughout Japan. Although Honda was geared to make 100 engines each month, Kitagawa curtailed its monthly production to between 50 and 80 units. Honda consequently suffered an inventory buildup, which caused a serious cash flow problem. An infuriated Fujisawa vowed to revamp the company's entire distribution system.

By 1952, the Honda Motor Company began manufacturing motorcycle frames, chains, and sprockets in addition to engines. Then, in a bold move, Fujisawa terminated the company's contract with Kitagawa and announced to its distributors, "We no longer will sell only our engines. If you want to do business with us, you must buy our entire motorcycle." For good reason, this decision upset distributors. The Kitagawa motorcycle bodies were more attractive than Honda's and had enjoyed immense popularity with the buying public. As a result, many distributors discontinued business with Honda. Fujisawa reacted quickly and established new and exclusive distributors in all of the vacated territories. This plan was the forerunner to a two-tier marketing system in which each distributor had an exclusive franchise in a given territory and, in turn, sold to retail dealers who had specific territories within the territory.

With the added manufacturing responsibilities, Honda's employment increased from 150 in 1951 to 1,337 by the end of 1952. Also during 1952, the company bought a sewing machine plant and converted it into a motorcycle manufacturing plant. It was during this same year that the company launched the Cub, a lightweight motorcycle that had little appeal to motorcyclists but did provide cheap and efficient transportation for the masses. The Cub reached a large, previously untapped market segment seeking a small, easy-to-operate vehicle that could be used by small businesses for local deliveries. With a step-through frame, automatic transmission, and one-hand controls, an operator could drive while carrying a package with his or her other hand. The Cub was ideal for moving small goods through the broken-down and overcrowded streets of Japan, but at the time, if it had been available in the United

States, it would have had only limited appeal as a "motorized bicycle," primarily driven for recreation.

For the first time in the young company's turbulent history, its manufacturing and marketing efforts were synchronized. While Soichiro Honda had furnished the engineering genius, Takeo Fujisawa had provided the marketing and administrative genius. Each man respected and had complete confidence in the other, and neither interfered with anything that fell within the scope of his partner's area of expertise. A perfect partnership had been born.

HONDA: THE MAVERICK COMPANY

With the new distribution system intact, the number of units sold jumped from 2,380 in 1951 to 9,659 in 1952. Sales skyrocketed to 29,797 in 1953, and hit 30,344 in 1954, the same year Honda Motor Company became a publicly owned corporation. Both Honda and Fujisawa believed that if the company had belonged only to their families, employees would have little motivation to work for them. They would have more incentive to work for the prosperity of their own organization.

Neither Honda nor Fujisawa had a college education, nor had they ever worked for the *zaibatsu,* the large family-dominated industrial and business combines that controlled Japanese industry before the General Headquarters of the U.S. Occupation Army abolished them at the end of World War II. The diversification of these powerful and influential organizations was similar to today's American multibillion dollar conglomerates. Because Honda wasn't involved with the zaibatsu, the establishment did not consider it a significant company, even though it was becoming a major force in the motorcycle industry. Honda was branded a maverick company and generally was shunned by the "old guard" members of the business community.

As far as the establishment was concerned, it was presumptuous for a company founded by a poor, uneducated mechanic to even think about being accepted among the ranks of Japan's elite business leaders. During the 1950s, while the company was growing by leaps and bounds, Honda operated with three large handicaps: (1) It had trouble recruiting top students from the major universities; (2) it lacked the proper "connections" with the banking community; and (3) it was not respected as an important company by Japanese governmental agencies, especially the powerful Ministry of International Trade and Industry (MITI). The influence and control of MITI combines the regulatory functions of the U.S. Department of Commerce, the Interstate Commerce Commission, and the U.S. Trade Representative.

It was MITI, for instance, that decreed how much production was permissible in Japan. When Honda filed an application for the construction of its Tokyo factory with a planned production of 300 units per month, suspicious MITI officials accused the company of beefing up its plans in order to obtain a larger allocation of gasoline. (It was MITI that allocated who received how much fuel.) Honda eventually received permission to construct the plant, but only after it had spent considerable time and effort maneuvering its way through a huge bureaucratic web. MITI also determined how many companies could operate within a specific industry, a factor that nearly prevented Honda's entry into the automobile industry (to be discussed later in this chapter). There is no doubt that the zaibatsu enjoyed preferred status with MITI, often at the expense of the small Johnny-come-lately companies such as Honda. Start-up enterprises received little encouragement, and in comparison to long-established firms, were treated as second-class citizens.

Soichiro Honda himself seemed to shun the establishment. He was viewed as a nonconformist in both his appearance and his attitudes. He often wore bright colors—he even owned a pink suit—and had been known to appear in his dirty overalls at important meetings with bankers.

During the company's early days, the first people hired rarely were those who had been college educated, and often were out-and-out rejects from other companies. Koichiro Yoshizawa, executive vice-president of Honda Motor Company in Tokyo, recalls joining the company upon graduating from college in 1954, "Honda was a small corporation and hardly known back then. I took examinations (written tests companies give to recruits) for several large manufacturing firms, but wasn't accepted—except by Honda, that is." Yoshizawa comments that Takeo Fujisawa "was an enthusiastic man who had a dream to help build an organization that was different from others in Japan, or, for that matter, anywhere else. He wanted to create a firm that had a spirit of a small- or medium-size company, an organization with individuals who could maintain their own vitality, an organization that could utilize the full resources of its people. I was drawn to Fujisawa because he made me want to share his dream."

Most Japanese employees are urged to subsume individual ambitions for the good of group goals. But Honda, as he had always done, rejected the accepted road. "First, each individual should work for himself—that's important," he said. "People will not sacrifice themselves for the company. They come to work at the company to enjoy themselves. That feeling would lead to innovation." Honda applied this credo to his own life. "The most important thing for me, is me."

Another young man who joined Honda in 1954 was Satoshi Okubo, who today serves as chairman of the board. "In the early fifties, there simply were not enough jobs available with the major corporations for everyone seeking jobs," Okubo explains. "I remember once when Mr. Honda addressed a group of new recruits, of which I was one, and he said, 'Other companies may not consider you to be the cream of the crop but we believe in you. Feel free to leave our company whenever you wish'—letting us know that if anyone was not satisfied and felt that a better opportunity existed somewhere else that he should take it." A smile flashes on Okubo's face and he adds, "It wasn't until I was thirty-five that I finally stopped looking in the newspapers for a job."

Honda's president and chief executive officer (CEO), Tadashi Kume, says, "After graduating from college as an engineer, I wanted to work for an automobile company, but those jobs were scarce and I failed almost all of the examinations. But I passed Honda's, so I settled to work for a motorcycle company." The CEO explains that he "never dreamed Honda would become the major company it is today. Nor did I believe that someday we'd manufacture automobiles."

That three of its highest ranked executives were rejected by other organizations illustrates the company's attitude. From its beginning, the Honda Motor Company showed no signs of following the precedents established by others. In fact, in comparison to other Japanese companies, a far less rigid organizational structure exists. To a great extent, the company's informal atmosphere is directly related to its founder, Soichiro Honda, a man who always felt more comfortable in a factory than in an office. And because he rubbed elbows in the plant with production workers—and dressed like them—he was always accessible. As Kume explains, "Mr. Honda was a great teacher, and most important, he listened to everyone's ideas. He constantly was asking everyone for their opinions, so consequently people felt comfortable expressing themselves." Unlike so many Japanese companies with rigid hierarchies, managers were and are quite accessible at Honda.

For years, the company's founder worked unassumingly in the laboratory, with a driving passion for perfection in engines. While over the years he became a legendary figure, in appearance Honda was no different from any other grease monkey in the shop. Honda attacked his work with such heated intensity that his quick temper frequently flared when things went wrong. He was known to rave and scream and was called *Kaminari-san*—"Mr. Thunder"—for his outbursts of temper. Once he reportedly hit a worker with a wrench in a fit of anger. Years later, Honda recalled, "Don't say I hit him. I touched him. In a way, it showed our closeness. And I thought he'd forgive me."

While his temper indicated he had little patience for mistakes and failures, he once said, "Many people dream of success. To me success can be achieved only through repeated failure and introspection. In fact, success represents the 1 percent of your work that results from the 99 percent that is called failure." Although those around him were well aware of his heated personality, these qualities mostly were overlooked.

People recognized that he was driven by an obsession and so could not accept failure. Soichiro Honda was a complex man; while he had a human side that quite visibly displayed his weaknesses, he also was a strong and determined leader. He was a man who inspired others to rally around him, and they, too, worked long, demanding hours.

As the Honda organization grew during the 1950s and into the following decade, so did its reputation for being a maverick company. During the years of the 1960s, Honda began to attract new employees from the universities in greater numbers. Even so, most were unlike those hired by the "establishment" companies. In Japan, the typical student from a major university would not dare consider a career with a "minor" company such as Honda. It was the independent graduate who sought employment with this maverick organization. Hence, like the man who founded the company, a different breed of Japanese youths began to join its ranks. And while Soichiro Honda has long since retired, the organization today is driven by managers who march as he and his partner did—to the beat of a different drummer.

BECOMING THE WORLD'S NUMBER ONE MOTORCYCLE COMPANY

The Honda Motor Company was in a fiercely competitive field during the early 1950s, but in a few short years it had zoomed to the top of the heap while others had fallen by the wayside. To a large degree, its success was due to the dual efforts of Honda and Fujisawa, a powerful one-two punch that gave the company a fighting edge over the competition.

With Fujisawa to concentrate on marketing and financing, Honda was able to develop the company's technology. Furthermore, Fujisawa clearly understood that no matter how strong the company's marketing organization was, its ultimate success would depend on selling a superior product. What was most unusual for a marketing person, however, was Fujisawa's insistence that Honda should create an independent research and development organization. This was officially established in 1957. With this autonomous posture, research and development (R&D) would have the freedom to work on long-term projects without the marketing and manufacturing demands for short-term profits.

Honda never gave up his passion for racing. So it wasn't long after the company had begun that he decided to test his technology in the world racing circuit. The company's first entry was in an international auto race held in Sao Paulo, Brazil, in early 1954. It was not a major race, but it was a start. The Honda team placed a disappointing thirteenth in a field of twenty-two. That June, Honda visited England to observe the Isle of Man Tourist Trophy Motorcycle Races and to get a feel for the international racing competition he would face. He was astonished to see that the motorcycles from such famous manufacturers as NSU of West Germany and Gilera of Italy raced at incredible speeds and had motors three times more powerful than his engines. He also observed that parts such as tires and chains were of higher quality than those made in Japan. The somewhat dismayed inventor returned home to his drawing board.

Two years after his trip abroad, Honda and his team of young engineers developed an engine comparable to those of the foreign competition. In 1955, Honda competed in the first All-Japan Motorcycle Endurance Road Race and captured first place in the 350-cc and 500-cc classes, but lost in the 125-cc and 150-cc division. In the second All-Japan Race in 1957, the company won only the 125-cc event. With these defeats Honda commented, "We should never imitate foreign technology. We must win through our own, no matter how hard it is to develop."

By the time Honda Motor Company participated in its first Isle of Man Race in 1959, the team was able to place sixth, seventh, and eighth in the 125-cc class, winning the manufacturer team prize. Two years later, the Honda team won the first five positions in both the 250-cc and 125-cc categories. England's *Daily Mirror* compared Honda's engines to "fine watches." Not only did these victories bring international attention to Honda products, which helped the marketing efforts, but the racing activities increased the company's techno-logical ability to make better motorcycles for the consumer. As one engineer comments, "It made us stretch and the result was that the quality of our products was greatly improved. We were able to adapt our technology for commercial motorcycles."

While his partner worked on building new and improved engines, Fujisawa focused on marketing. Although he appreciated the value of the company's racing activities, Fujisawa believed that large, heavy motorcycles had a limited market compared to the smaller models that handled more easily and could be used for more practical purposes. "Can you use what you've learned about racing to come up with an inexpensive, safe-looking motorcycle that can be driven with one hand?" he challenged Honda. Fujisawa foresaw a much larger market than the one that catered to motorcycle enthusiasts. He wanted to sell an easy-to-handle, inexpensive, safe-looking motorcycle that could be used by the large number of commercial establishments in Japan for running errands and delivering small packages. He also envisioned the company reaching yet another expansive, untapped market: the Japanese wife, who was responsible for the family's grocery shopping.

In 1958, Honda introduced the 50-cc Supercub. It had an automatic clutch, three-speed transmission, and automatic starter. What's more, it had the safe, friendly appearance of a bicycle. Its step-through frame made it especially convenient for female riders. Nobody could have anticipated its tremendous reception. The Supercub was an incredible success—the company was inundated with orders, so many, in fact, that Honda decided to "bet the mortgage" on this model: The company built a highly automated, 30,000-unit-per-month manufacturing plant—a manufacturing capacity nearly ten times greater than the previous year's sales! It was a tremendous gamble, but it paid off. The demand was so great that by 1959, the Supercub accounted for 168,000 of the 285,000 units the company sold. The model had pushed Honda to the top of the summit. At the time of the Supercub's introduction, Japan had fifty motorcycle manufacturers. Ten years later, this number dwindled to only four, with Honda as Japan's num-

ber one motorcycle manufacturer—a title it has never relin-
quished.

Fujisawa's marketing genius again surfaced. Using the
Supercub's popularity, he revamped Honda's channels of distribution. By positioning the Supercub as "something much
more like a bicycle than a motorcycle," the company began
selling its prized new model directly to retailers, primarily
Japan's more than 12,000 small bicycle shops. This time
Fujisawa bypassed the two-tier distribution system and, most
important, he installed a cash-on-delivery policy, giving the
company more control over its dealerships than its competitors, who operated on consignment.

By 1961, Honda's motorcycle sales hit 100,000 units a month,
an unprecedented number. Honda was a winner with the consumer and was consistently winning in the racing circuit as
well. It was time to seek new challenges in perhaps the world's
most competitive arena: the automobile industry.

MAKING THE TRANSITION FROM
MOTORCYCLES TO AUTOMOBILES

Only a decade or so after having entered the field, Honda was
recognized as the world's leader in the motorcycle industry, a
truly miraculous feat. By 1960, the company was equally determined to achieve the impossible a second time. While the
Honda Motor Company had become the dominant force in
what was considered one of the most glamorous growth industries of post-World War II, that achievement was child's play
compared to entering the automobile industry. The field was
a highly mature industry, one that required an enormous capital investment. Honda was still a relatively small company
compared to the multibillion dollar automobile manufacturers, the industrial giants of the world. Furthermore, Honda's
success in building motorcycles seemed to have little bearing
on its ability to make cars. The dominant companies appeared
to have progressed too far to permit a Johnny-come-lately to
join their ranks. In the 1960s, it was perhaps the least accessible industry in the world.

Starting an automobile company is an extremely bold venture. The last person to succeed in the United States was Walter P. Chrysler, in 1925. The graveyard of American auto makers who have failed is studded with such names as Hudson, Studebaker, Packard, Kaiser, Willys, Tucker, and scores of lesser-known entrepreneurs. The most recent attempt by an American was John Z. De Lorean's. He formed De Lorean Motor Company in 1975. Until his failure to launch his sleek DMC-12, De Lorean, a former GM group vice-president, was perhaps the most celebrated automobile personality in the United States.

Making matters worse was Honda's battle with MITI, which wanted to merge Japan's ten auto makers into three groups, with the nation's two automobile leaders, Toyota and Nissan, emerging as international giants, and the mini-car manufacturers as the third group. There was also pending legislation in Japan to prohibit new firms from manufacturing four-wheel vehicles. Honda vehemently resisted MITI's merger proposals. "Government officials should always act to protect the public interest," he said, "but they tend to become an obstacle when you try to do something new." One of MITI's biggest fears was that Japan had opened its doors to American car imports, and it felt its weak and fragmented auto industry could not compete with the likes of the formidable General Motors, Ford, and Chrysler.

Soichiro Honda, a staunch believer in free competition, vehemently opposed MITI's attempt to place arbitrary limits on his company. "If you want to control us," a furious Honda told the government, "you will have to be a shareholder. Only our shareholders have the right to dictate to the management of this organization. Only then will we listen to you!" In a rushed effort to get its entry under the wire before the legislation passed, the company reacted more quickly than it originally planned and introduced its S-360 model, a sports car sometimes described as "a motorcycle with four wheels and a roof." In the end, MITI's proposed legislation was defeated.

All too frequently, American industrialists are quick to attribute the success achieved by Japanese industry to "unfair"

government intervention. Lee Iacocca, the Chrysler CEO, minced few words when discussing the need for American free enterprise to adapt to

> a new world that now includes a formidable rival, Japan, and a world where nobody else is playing by the rules of pure laissez-faire. . . . The field where this game is being played is not level. Instead, it's strongly tilted in favor of Japan. As a result, we're playing with one hand tied behind our back. . . . Japanese industry is not playing by itself. It's backed to the hilt in its close relationship to the Japanese government in the form of MITI, the Ministry of International Trade and Industry. MITI's job is to determine the industries that are critical to Japan's future and to help out in their research and development.

The facts, however, show that Honda has never benefited from government support. In fact, MITI officials were extremely uncooperative, and went so far as to claim that the company's fast-growth strategy "bordered on insanity." "I probably would have been even more successful had we not had MITI," Soichiro Honda says. "MITI was incapable of making automobiles, but I was capable."

Applying the same strategy it used to achieve technological excellence in building motorcycles, Honda entered the automobile racing circuit. And Honda's autonomous R&D company was given the freedom to focus on the development of superior automotive products and enjoy the luxury of not being concerned with short-term gains. Its engineers were permitted to take bold chances.

Shortly after the company started building automobiles, its founder announced that the company would build a racing car that would win the Le Mans. While some people thought his announcement bordered on madness, Honda had a good reason for making it: He knew that by telling the world of his plans to build the world's fastest racing car, the company was bound to attract exceptional engineers. One such engineer was Shoichiro Irimajiri, a motorcycle enthusiast who joined the company immediately after he graduated from the prestigious

Tokyo University's College of Engineering in 1963. Irimajiri had wanted to be an aeronautical engineer, but in the early 1960s, Japanese manufacturers were doing more repairing than building of airplanes. After reading a small article in a local newspaper that said Soichiro Honda might consider building a small airplane, Irimajiri contacted the company for a job interview. "I was impressed that Yoshio Nakamura, a famous aeronautical engineer during World War II, had joined the company. Another person who influenced my decision was Akira Sono, a 1961 Tokyo University graduate who worked for Honda R&D. Then upon meeting Mr. Honda, my mind was made up that this was the right company for me."

Irimajiri, president of Honda of America Manufacturing, Inc., began as an engineer on the auto racing team. He often ran into the company's founder, who worked closely with the racing efforts. "Although I was just a young engineer, Mr. Honda constantly would look over my shoulder and ask me questions about my drawings. 'What is this?' and 'What is your intention for this drawing?' he would ask. Although he had no formal training, he immediately would point out defects in my design. He would comment, 'It looks too weak' or 'That looks too heavy.' While in the beginning, I'd think he was mistaken, after I recalculated I'd find out that he was right."

Irimajiri recalls one particular incident that illustrates how demanding Honda was of his engineers. "I was responsible for designing our engine's piston for a British Grand Prix race that we lost in August 1965. The engine was sent back to our R&D department for study, and Mr. Honda personally supervised the teardown of the engine. 'Who designed this burned piston?' he demanded. I stepped forward to confess, and he ordered me to bring him both the old and the new drawings immediately. I laid out both drawings and he studied them.

" 'Why did you make these changes?' he demanded.

"I had made a drastic reduction in the weight of the piston and believed my design was carefully backed up by various calculations and evaluations of past data. So I confidently explained my theory to him—and he exploded. 'Who do you think you're talking to? I designed and made that! And I have years of experience in the piston manufacturing business.'

"The more I hemmed and hawed, the madder he became. 'You! Stupid! No wonder the piston gets burned. You have changed the thickness here.'

" 'I understand that about 70 percent of the piston heat is dispersed through the piston rings,' I stuttered, but with conviction. 'Therefore, I think the design change doesn't have anything to do with the overheating.'

"When Mr. Honda heard this, he turned into an angry fireball. 'You fool! I hate college graduates! They use only their heads. Do you really think you can use such obsolete data obtained from old, low performance engines? I have been making and working with pistons for more than twenty years. I am fully aware how critical half a millimeter is here. A company doesn't need people like you who use only their heads. Before you laid out this design, why didn't you go check the pistons yourself and listen to opinions of those experienced people in the shop? If you think college academics is everything, you are totally wrong. You will be useless here at Honda unless you spend more time being on the spot for many years to come.'

"With that, he told me to take the piston around to every person in the machining and casting shops who had worked on it and apologize for my mistake. To add to my embarrassment, Mr. Honda followed me as I made the rounds."

Honda eventually enjoyed many successes in the automobile racing arena. Later in 1965, the Honda team had its first Formula I victory when it won the Mexican Grand Prix. In the meantime, Honda continued to win racing events on the motorcycle circuit, capturing all five solo World Championships (50-cc, 125-cc, 250-cc, 350-cc and 500-cc classes) in 1966, marking the first time one company was victorious in all races. That same year Honda set a world record of eleven consecutive Formula II victories for smaller cars, and the following September the company won the Italian Formula I Grand Prix.

In 1968, the company abruptly withdrew from Formula I

competition for several years so its engineers could concentrate on creating a nonpolluting car. Honda had its breakthrough in 1973 when it introduced the Compound Vortex Controlled Combustion (CVCC) engine in its Honda Civic. The CVCC became the first engine to comply with emission standards set by the 1970 U.S. Clean Air Act—and the only one to do so without a catalytic converter.

Development of the CVCC began in early 1971, and although it ultimately put Honda in the automobile industry limelight, the program was almost scrapped before it got off the ground. Tadashi Kume, Honda's current CEO, was chief engineer of Honda R&D. But at age thirty-nine he resigned after he had failed to convince Honda's bullheaded founder that the company should switch from air-cooled to water-cooled engines. Several days later, Kume was lured back with the promise that he and a group of other engineers, known within the organization as the "all-or-nothing team," could work on a new water-cooled engine. They worked day and night on what they believed was the company's only opportunity to gain a foothold in the competitive automobile industry. With immense dedication, they achieved their goal, and by the end of the year the team had come through with a technological triumph—the revolutionary CVCC engine. Soichiro Honda obviously was proud of the engineering team's success when he congratulated them and humbly said, "Air-cooling is the limit of my experience."

Tetsuo Chino, currently president of Honda North America, Inc., recalls an unusual predicament he faced in 1963 during his second year with the company. "The company was led by two strong men: Mr. Honda, who provided the engineering genius, and Mr. Fujisawa, who provided the marketing and administrative genius. It was a difficult time of transition for us because our government was trying to restrict the number of auto makers in Japan. So we felt forced to get into the business quickly. To do so, we built a small, chain-driven sports car that really was based on our motorcycle technology.

"Mr. Fujisawa had a broader vision of the market, and if the only automobile that Mr. Honda would give him would be a sports car, then that's what he'd use to penetrate a larger market. I was in marketing and reported to Mr. Fujisawa, so he told me to design a display for the new car, the S-500, to present at the upcoming 1963 Tokyo Auto Show. Following his orders, I positioned it as a business-commuter car. His reasoning was, of course, to appeal to a larger market.

"But when Mr. Honda saw my plans, he called me to his office and demanded to know what I was trying to do. His demand required no answer because when he was angry, one did not try to reason with him. Mr. Honda made it perfectly clear that the S-500 was to be a sports car. So there I was—a young man, just starting a career, and I found myself caught between the two cofounders of the company. Knowing that both of them would attend the show, I knew if I didn't think of something, one surely would be upset with me!

"My solution was to design two displays and put them at opposite ends of the display area—one showing the car as a sports car and the other showing it as an executive's car. Mr. Honda and Mr. Fujisawa visited the show separately, and I carefully took each one to his own corner—not showing Mr. Honda the business display and not showing Mr. Fujisawa the sports car display. As I later found out, they both knew what I did, but neither ever said a word about it to me or to each other. They had that kind of special partnership—each had great respect for the other, so they secretly were pleased because I handled the situation in a manner that avoided a possible confrontation. In the end, it turned out that they were both right, because today Honda is in both markets."

2

Honda Comes
to America

IN 1958, a group formed to study overseas marketplaces elected to bypass the United States altogether. Following visits to virtually all noncommunist countries, the group report recommended that Honda's first efforts in foreign expansion should be directed at Europe and Southeast Asia, the latter because of its proximity to Japan. The report revealed that while most Americans had sufficient disposable incomes, there would be little demand for lightweight, Japanese motorcycles. What's more, the U.S. motorcycle market was declining.

Takeo Fujisawa refused to accept the report. Believing that the American consumer was the pacesetter of products sold on an international scale, he reminded the group members about a Honda philosophy that demanded the company "face the toughest challenges first." With this in mind, he insisted, "We must attempt to penetrate the difficult U.S. market *before* we go elsewhere." It was an if-we-can-make-it-in-America-we-can-make-it-anywhere attitude. And if the efforts failed, the company then could regroup and start over in accordance with the group's recommendation.

Many considered Fujisawa's decision another example of Honda's maverick approach. Other Japanese companies usually marketed their products in nearby Taiwan and Thailand, using them as testing grounds to judge foreign acceptance.

Only afterward did these companies consider entering the European and American markets. But then other Japanese motorcycle manufacturers had done poorly in Southeast Asian markets where there were poor roads and little disposable income. And while the European market looked interesting, it was heavily dominated by its own established motorcycle makers.

After the decision was made, the Japanese Ministry of Finance had to approve Honda's application to invest in the U.S. market. That same year, Japan's largest auto maker, Toyota, failed to successfully introduce the Toyopet in the United States. How could Honda possibly hope to succeed? Processing the application took five months, but the Ministry finally approved it. Although the company had requested permission to capitalize its American venture with $1 million, the Ministry permitted Honda to take only $250,000 out of Japan. And only half of this amount could be in cash, with the balance in inventory. Once more Honda was forced to operate with a severe handicap—again courtesy of the Japanese government.

A DIFFERENCE IN CULTURES

To best understand the cultural differences between the United States and Japan, the Japanese word *mottainai* must be understood. Its definition is that all things are precious, and to waste is a sin. The contrasts between Japan and the United States are striking: Japan is a land of limited resources, and the United States is a land of plenty that has evolved into a disposable society.

Japan is an overcrowded land about the size of California with a population of 122 million. Because of its jagged, mountainous terrain, only 17 percent of the land is habitable. Its population density of 318 people per square kilometer is 15 times that of the United States and 3.5 times that of China. Japan's population is slightly more than half the U.S. population, but in an area about 1/25 the size. With vast shortages in both natural resources and real estate, the Japanese think, live, and work differently. The awareness of space, or the lack thereof, has been deeply engrained into the Japanese culture. By the early 1600s, nearly 400 years ago, Japan was already afflicted with a population density almost twice that of the present-day United States. (To look at it another way, if Japan today had the same population density as the United States, there would be only 8 million Japanese.)

The shortage of space caused late-nineteenth-century farmers in Japan to work collectively to improve efficiency. This teamwork approach formed the basis of the consensus management system that prevails in Japanese business circles as the twenty-first century approaches. The Japanese usually establish a strong identity as part of a group (that is, a family, corporation, nation). A large Japanese corporation often is considered more than just a place to work and to generate profits.

In contrast, during the nineteenth century adventurous Americans pioneered a vast virgin land, building farms and ranches often miles from the nearest neighbor. Isolated, these settlers became fiercely independent—a characteristic that epitomizes the American spirit today.

Another obvious and significant difference in cultures is Japan's homogeneous society. Conversely, America is a melting pot of diverse races and nationalities living together in a country that only a little more than a decade ago celebrated its 200th birthday. America is a young society in comparison to Japan, and that sometimes fosters confrontations. Americans are more outspoken, so it is no surprise that confrontations in the United States are resolved by a battery of attorneys. California, for example, has more attorneys than the entire country of Japan.

Americans who cling to the national heritage of rugged individualism like to argue that group-oriented societies stifle competitiveness. But the Japanese educational system must be considered the exception. For despite the social molding process to which they are subjected, the academic competition among Japanese elementary- and secondary-school students is savage in its intensity—so much so that it makes the battle for grades waged in even the most competitive U.S. school look like a game of pattycake. This intensely competitive spirit is also evident in Japan's business arena.

These differences existed long before 1959 and compounded the obstacles that Honda faced when it embarked on its bold venture to the shores of a faraway new land. It was not only the great distance of this planet's largest ocean that separated the two nations but the cultural differences as well.

BREAKING THE ICE IN THE UNITED STATES

The group leader who recommended bypassing the United States and exporting instead to Southeast Asia was Kihachiro Kawashima. After joining the company in 1951, he worked under Fujisawa during the early developmental stages of the motorcycle sales network in Japan. In 1958, Kawashima was named chief of the Special Planning Division, in charge of exploring the possibility of exporting motorcycles to other markets. While heading the group, Kawashima continued to work in Honda's domestic sales organization. After Fujisawa overruled the decision and chose to enter the American market, he immediately named the thirty-nine-year-old Kawashima to the top position of the newly formed American marketing organization.

To outsiders, Fujisawa's selection was a peculiar one. After all, Kawashima was not in favor of entering the U.S. market. However, the decision was made by consensus. So although he initially voiced opposition, after a consensus was reached, Kawashima pledged his alliance with enthusiasm and vigor. The choice of Kawashima was largely a result of his past experiences with Fujisawa in establishing motorcycle dealerships throughout Japan.

At the time, nearly all exporting from Japan was done through the centuries-old influential and rich *sogoshosha*, commonly known as trading companies. So when Honda announced its plans to enter the U.S. market, it naturally was assumed that it would work through a trading company. Fujisawa, however, didn't believe trading companies were capable of handling motorcycles that required service and parts.

Instead of taking the traditional trading company route, the plan was for Honda to establish its own distributorship. This was in line with Honda's philosophy of keeping its independence and not relying on others to determine its destiny. When word got out about Honda's plans, a long-established U.S. motorcycle distributor approached the company and said it would be willing to carry the line.

> During the course of conversation, Fujisawa mentioned that Honda intended initially to send 7,500 units.
>
> "That's a lot, and I doubt if it's possible," the distributing company president said. He added, after a brief pause, "Don't you think you're being overly optimistic to expect to sell so many during your first year?"
>
> "I was talking about 7,500 a month," Fujisawa said.
>
> "A month! Even BSA and Triumph sell only 6,000 a year in the United States."
>
> With that reply, Fujisawa announced that Honda would not work through a distributor. "If people in the motorcycle business in America think so small," he said, "then we should establish our own distribution system there."

In late 1958, Kawashima and an assistant arrived in San Francisco to explore the potential marketplace in the United States. From the Golden Gate City, they traveled to cities across the country. "My first reaction to America," Kawashima recalls, "was how big and wealthy a country it was. I kept thinking that had the Japanese government known what I knew, they never would have entered a war with the United States." Upon returning to Tokyo, Kawashima reported that there were 3,000 motorcycle dealers in the United States, with only a third of them open five days a week. The remainder were part-timers who worked in the evenings and on weekends. There were also 450,000 annual motorcycle registrations in the United States, 60,000 of which involved European imports. His report noted that inventories were low, dealers bought on consignment, retailers provided consumer financing, and after-the-sale service was poor.

In June 1959, American Honda Motor Co. was formed. That same month, Kihachiro Kawashima, its newly appointed president, and two young assistants, Takayuki Kobayashi and Shozo Yamagishi, arrived in Los Angeles. The three enthusiastic men truly believed they would succeed against all odds because they carried the Honda philosophy that the company founders had fostered. As Kawashima explains, "We had no specific strategy except to see what we could do in America, and we received authority to communicate directly to Mr. Fujisawa. In the beginning, he never gave us a target to shoot for. There was no discussion about profits or even a deadline for break-even. Fujisawa said only, 'If anyone could succeed, I know you could.'"

The three men chose Los Angeles because it had a large Japanese community, a warm climate for motorcycling, and was on the west coast, nearer to Japan than the rest of the country. They rented an $80-a-month apartment with only one bed, so two men had to sleep on the floor. After leasing a warehouse in a run-down section of the city, they pushed and piled motorcycle crates three-high by hand to keep expenses down. They also swept the floors and built and maintained a parts bin. As Kawashima tells, "It was something that we had to do, so we did it."

Initially, they placed ads in motorcycle trade magazines, and made store-to-store calls to motorcycle retailers. In the beginning, the reception was poor, mainly because of the men's broken English. Of course, the three men also were confronted with strange social customs and a confusing legal system. By the end of the first six months, the three men set up only fifteen dealerships and sales mounted to a mere 200 units. Apparently the American distributor who said Honda couldn't sell 7,500 units a year was right.

Much of the first six months' failure resulted because Honda failed to realize that the American motorcycle business runs from April through August. The company had arrived in the United States in June, close to the end of the 1959 season. To get off to a fresh start in January 1960, Kawashima used a small advertising campaign that consisted mainly of small ads in trade motorcycle magazines. These ads served two purposes: First, readers inquired at local dealerships about Honda, in turn, arousing dealers' curiosity about the company; second, the responses resulted in sales. By spring, forty dealers were carrying the larger Honda motorcycles. For a while business looked as if it was picking up. Then, in April, the bottom fell out.

Complaints came pouring in from dealers and consumers that the motorcycle engines were leaking oil and having clutch failures. "We couldn't believe it," Kawashima explains. "We had great confidence in our product, and here our reputation in America was practically destroyed before we could get started. Mr. Honda gave us a guarantee that we had an international product, and right before our eyes our motorcycles were malfunctioning."

The company had failed to realize that motorcycles in the United States were driven differently than in Japan. With this country's open spaces and wide roads, Americans rode their motorcycles at greater speeds and for longer distances than the Japanese. Consequently, motorcycles were air-freighted back to Honda's testing laboratory in Japan, causing further drain on the low cash reserves of the new enterprise. During April, engineers worked around the clock testing the defective motorcycles, analyzing why they malfunctioned and what corrections were necessary to compensate for the different conditions. By the end of the month, the head gasket and clutch spring were redesigned, road tests were made, and the problems were solved.

In addition to the mechanical difficulties, another near-disaster occurred. Following the signing of a new security treaty between Japan and the United States in January 1960, Japanese law required that it be ratified by the National Diet. However, leftist forces opposed maintaining close ties with the United States and demanded that Japan be neutral. The treaty caused a heated debate, and as a consequence, workers and students demonstrated daily around the National Diet building. U.S. Press Secretary James C. Hagerty arrived in Tokyo on June 10, ahead of President Dwight D. Eisenhower (whose visit was the first ever for an American president while in office), and was met by a large student demonstration. The incident created some anti-Japanese sentiment in the United States, and as a result, several dealers canceled their orders with Honda.

Meanwhile, back in the United States something good and unexpected happened. The three men used the 50-cc Supercubs in the Los Angeles area to do errands because they had only one car among them. To their surprise, the Supercubs attracted a lot of attention. "When we first came to the United States, we didn't want to sell our little bikes," Kawashima explains. "Even though the Supercub was a huge success in Japan, we believed that it would hurt our image in the United States because we believed Americans were in love with power and speed. Naturally, we went after the big bike market. The Supercub definitely was not macho. We didn't want to alienate the motorcycle dealers who catered to the black-leather-jacket customers.

"Soon we were driving the Supercubs everywhere we went in Los Angeles and people would ask so many questions about them. From the comments we received, we began to get the feeling the small bike might have some great sales potential in this country after all."

Once Honda decided to make a concentrated effort to market the Supercub in the United States, it followed a strategy similar to the one Fujisawa had developed in Japan. But in America, the salespeople started calling on a variety of retailers, not just motorcycle dealers who sold the big, powerful bikes from dirty and oily shops. By selling the small bikes in nicer shops, customers who didn't frequent the garage-type outlets were exposed to Honda products. Two company-owned stores were opened, in Phoenix, Arizona, and San Francisco. These were clean and attractive stores, and Honda store employees were instructed to wear ties. In fact, Honda recommended that independent dealers wear ties too. While Honda sold directly to bicycle shops throughout Japan, in the United States its sales force contacted all conceivable retailers, including sporting goods stores, hobby shops, lawn-mower repair shops, supermarkets, hardware stores, and even several college bookstores.

As Kawashima points out, "At first we worked under the principle 'when in Rome, do as the Romans do,' and we approached only dealers who had previous motorcycle experience. But then we discovered that other retailers were fair game, too, so we went after them and brought new blood into the industry."

The sales pitch was low-key. A Honda sales representative typically would approach a potential retailer to sell the brightly colored Supercub 50-cc step-through scooters and would be asked, "What are they?"

"Just try 'em out for a couple of weeks and see how they ride. I'll be back later," the salesman would reply, and he'd leave.

The retailer would discover that the new products were quite different from the typical motorcycles that often leaked oil. The Supercub was small and good-looking and attracted a lot of attention. It could be displayed in clean showrooms like a car, and took up a small amount of space. When the salesman would return, he'd hear, "These things are great. I want to handle them."

Honda soon was flying its bigger dealers to Japan to learn about the company's philosophy. In particular, the dealers were told that "good service is the key to long-term success." Until a parts distribution system could be set up, parts had to be air freighted from Japan to American Honda and on to the dealer. Even though it was an expensive way to do business in the short run, the company jumped through hoops to let America know the name Honda was synonomous with good service. By the end of 1961, there were 500 dealers in the United States, and 150 Honda employees worked out of three zone offices in Los Angeles, Wisconsin, and New Jersey. Company representatives traveled the country on caravan tours, conducting mini-conventions, promoting and demonstrating Honda products. Dealers also were being taught how to handle a new breed of customers who weren't the grease-monkey types who repaired their own bikes. The new customers ranged from students to professionals. For the first time in the United States, women were buying motor bikes. It wasn't that Honda had abandoned selling its big motorcycles; instead, the company had created an entirely new market.

"YOU MEET THE NICEST PEOPLE ON A HONDA"

By early 1963, Honda still was working with its original Los Angeles advertising agency, which promoted both small and big motorcycles equally. All ads were carefully drafted so they wouldn't offend either consumer group. Then in the spring of 1963, while business was humming triumphantly, the company decided to commit $5 million to a strong advertising campaign. But this time Honda would work with a large, national ad agency. Grey Advertising had made several presentations trying to land the Honda account when a UCLA instructor submitted a report that one of his advertising students had written as a class assignment. It was an ad campaign for Honda with the theme: "You Meet the Nicest People on a Honda." Grey purchased the student's idea and took it to Honda.

Honda, however, nearly rejected it. When the campaign was presented to Honda's American management team, which had grown from three to five by 1963, both Kawashima and the company's treasurer favored working with another agency's proposal. But Honda's sales director's strong conviction in favor of the Grey presentation finally persuaded the others to go along with the "Nicest People" theme. It was Grey who did the famous Greyhound Bus ad: "It's Such a Comfort to Take the Bus and Leave the Driving to Us," and its success influenced Honda in making its choice.

The campaign placed ads in many of America's most widely read and prestigious magazines such as *Life, Look,* and the *Saturday Evening Post.* Ads also were on radio, television, billboards, and in dealer newspapers across the country. Everyday middle-class people were shown riding Hondas. It was one of the most successful advertising campaigns in history.

The black-leather-jacket image that Marlon Brando helped create in the popular movie *The Wild Ones* was changed practically overnight. No longer was it taboo to be seen driving a motorcycle.

By the end of 1963, more than 100,000 Honda units had been sold in the United States, outselling all domestic and foreign manufacturers combined. By 1964, Honda had captured nearly 50 percent of the entire American motorcycle market. That same year, Honda announced that its products no longer would be sold on a consignment basis; instead dealers would be required to pay cash on delivery. While nearly every dealer balked, not a single dealership agreement was discontinued. For the first time in the history of the motorcycle field, a manufacturer, not the dealer, was in the driver's seat. Within a few years, every motorcycle manufacturer had followed suit. Honda had revolutionized the entire industry.

MAKING THE AMERICAN TRANSITION FROM MOTORCYCLES TO CARS

Although the company was the number one seller of motorcycles in the United States by the mid-1960s, it was by no means a "given" that Americans would automatically run out to buy Honda automobiles. Unlike the fragmented motorcycle industry where there was relatively easy access, the capital-intensive American automobile industry was dominated by the "Big Three," with General Motors ranking as the world's number one industrial company and with Ford and Chrysler not far behind. A Honda bike was a fun product, but not a serious purchase as was an automobile. And Honda's history as a motorcycle manufacturer didn't carry a great deal of weight— there was less reason to buy a car from a motorcycle maker than there was to buy a television set from a radio manufacturer. Honda could count on few crossovers from satisfied motorcycle customers. To crack the competitive car business in the United States, Honda had to develop new strategies.

In some respects, Honda actually was hindered by its reputation for being the world's leading motorcycle manufacturer.

Many auto dealers considered the first Honda N600 models shipped to Hawaii in 1969 and the following year to the U.S. mainland as "overgrown motorcycles" rather than cars. In the beginning, Honda sold cars only in Hawaii, California, Oregon, and Washington.

Most important, automobiles had an entirely different distribution system than motorcycles. To find automobile dealers was difficult. Unlike dealers selling the small bikes, a car dealer couldn't simply be told, "Keep one for a few weeks and I'll be back to see how you do with it."

And while Honda was able to apply much of its marketing know-how from Japan to sell motorcycles, this was not the case with automobiles. Automobile sales in the United States during the late 1960s were far different from the automobile business in Japan. For example, the company had entered the field so far behind Toyota and Nissan that good retail locations no longer were available in Japan. The large areas that did remain were so prohibitively expensive that it was not feasible to use them as dealerships. Consequently, Honda to this day has a network of small dealerships in Japan, many with only one or two cars displayed in the showroom. In Japan, it is also common practice for car salespeople to call on prospects in their homes, a routine that occurs mostly during the evening. In addition, many cars traded in with the purchase of a new model are turned over to a Honda Motor Company subsidiary for resale. Because of the space shortage, the automobile maker, not the dealer, owns and operates many of the service centers.

As stated earlier, the scarcity of land in Japan has had a strong impact on the country's culture and on its business practices. In the United States, some state laws govern the distances between an auto maker's dealerships: California law, for example, requires a distance of no less than 10 miles. No such restrictions exist in Japan. So while the early distribution of motorcycles in the United States was like Honda's in Japan, the selling of automobiles in the two countries had no such similarities.

The company realized that only a small percentage of its

motorcycle dealers were good automobile dealer prospects, and accordingly, picked and chose only those with the business acumen and financial capacity to succeed. In these cases, the company required separate sales centers—Honda did not wish to mix cars and motorcycles. There were a handful of automobile dealers scattered across the country who believed in Honda technology because of the company's proven track record with motorcycles, and a few did come aboard in the beginning.

Setting up a distribution system in the United States was a slow process. The dealerships were established one at a time. For the most part, it was a matter of convincing a Chevrolet or Ford dealer, for example, to place one or two N600s in the corner of the showroom. Rarely would a dealer carry the Honda line exclusively. Instead, a "Big Three" dealership would have a foreign car department. It wasn't until the mid-1970s that Honda finally was able to deal from strength and insist that dealers sell its cars exclusively.

The single factor that helped establish the company's reputation for automobile quality in the United States more than any other was Honda's 1973 introduction of the compound vortex controlled combustion (CVCC) engine. While most people did not understand its engineering, they did recognize that the subcompact Civic got good mileage on leaded gasoline—and an expensive catalytic converter wasn't required to meet the tough emission standards set by the 1970 U.S. Clean Air Act. The CVCC, with its low-emission system based on the conventional four-stroke reciprocating engine, was Honda's answer to air pollution, which at the time was a major concern to the automotive industry in the United States. The CVCC differed from conventional engines because it did not require a catalytic converter to lessen the amount of carbon monoxide, unburned hydrocarbons, and oxides of nitrogen in the exhaust of internal combustion engines. Instead it employed a lean overall mixture and regulated its combustion to suppress production of the unwanted pollutants. As the only automotive manufacturer to accomplish this, Honda was viewed as an innovative company.

By 1975, Honda was selling 10,000 Civics a month. The following year, Honda brought out the larger Accord, which was named *Motor Trend* magazine's "Import Car of the Year." At $3,995, a highly competitive sticker price for a car of its size and quality, the demand was so great that Honda dealers had customers waiting their turns to buy one.

In a matter of five years, Honda cars had gained acceptance in the competitive U.S. market. As executive vice-president and former American Honda president Koichiro Yoshizawa explains, "Americans are more willing to try a new product than the Japanese, who belong to a more traditional and ritualistic society. Although we knew it would be difficult to break into the U.S. market, we were patient and bided our time. Of course, the key to success in the American marketplace is to provide quality and good service."

3

Honda:
Made in the U.S.A.

IN 1974, when sales of Honda automobiles in the United States were beginning to show some promise, Honda's management in Japan began discussing the feasibility of building a plant in the United States. This was a time when there wasn't yet any talk about restricting imports. What prompted the feasibility study was the demand for Honda products coupled with the fact that its Japanese factories were operating at near full capacity. Unless a new factory was built, it would be difficult for Honda to produce additional units.

At the time, when the yen was weak against the dollar, good business judgment dictated building a new plant on domestic soil, where Japanese labor could create high-quality products at competitive prices. To many, it would seem foolhardy for a small company like Honda to go up against GM, Ford, and Chrysler on their home turf in the United States. But Honda, in line with its philosophy to manufacture its products in the markets where they are sold, boldly decided to build a U.S. factory. Today, there are sixty-six Honda plants throughout the world, in such countries as Belgium, Brazil, Canada, China, France, India, Indonesia, Italy, Korea, Mexico, New Zealand, Nigeria, Peru, the Philippines, and Thailand.

Building a U.S. factory was a bold decision; the only other foreign auto maker to build on American soil at the time was Volkswagen, which was struggling to establish a manufacturing plant in Pennsylvania. And the question of whether Americans could build products with the same quality as the Japanese was unresolved (the general feeling was that the American Volkswagen workers could not match their German counterparts).

At the time it decided to build in the United States, Honda already had become the number one company in motorcycle sales. But the company had been in the U.S. automobile market only four years, and while the 1974 feasibility study projected that the company could produce 100,000 cars a year in the United States, in the previous year Honda's American sales reached only 40,000 units, all Civics, the only car Honda offered. Both the Americans and the Japanese considered Honda a small automobile company, and comments echoed off both sides of the Pacific that Honda's plans were audacious. Some hinted that Honda should build the new plant as a joint venture with another auto maker, but that wasn't Honda's style; Honda philosophy dictated that the company must always carry its own torch. As Honda Motor Company president Tadashi Kume explains: "There are times when the hard numbers and the hard facts say no, don't do these things, but we do them anyway because they coincide with our philosophy."

The company decided first to build a 260,000-square-foot factory to produce motorcycles. Doing so would require a $30 million investment, which, although a large sum, would not have bankrupted the company. And it was a small amount of money compared to the cost of building an automobile factory. The plan was to "test the waters," and if the motorcycle production was successful, the company would expand the plant to build automobiles as well. The company felt that the worst possible scenario would be to forfeit the $30 million and rely on Japanese production only. It was a scenario, however, that Honda simply wouldn't accept.

THE GREAT SEARCH FOR A
BUILDING SITE

In April 1976, a brief wire story from Tokyo appeared in the *Columbus Citizen-Journal*. The article said a Japanese automobile company was conducting a feasibility study on building a plant in the United States, but no company was named. James Duerk, then the Ohio development director, read the article with interest, carefully folded it, and placed it in his briefcase.

That morning, he walked into Governor James A. Rhodes's office and handed the clipping to him. "What do you think, Governor? Perhaps we ought to go to Japan within the next few weeks and check this out."

The governor read the article and, after a slight pause, said, "We'll go tomorrow. Set it up."

Duerk contacted a Japanese consulate officer in Chicago to get the visas, then arranged for the State Department to schedule meetings in Japan with top auto makers. The two men left at nine o'clock the following morning and arrived on the emperor's birthday, a national holiday, that fell on a Saturday. On Sunday and Monday, Rhodes and Duerk met with the executive vice-president of Toyota, the chairman of the board of Nissan, and the president of Honda. Rhodes and Duerk made a strong pitch for Ohio and passed out a package of materials on the state's work force, location, taxes, environmental laws, and transportation system. The trip lasted less than five days.

Months followed without word from any of the three companies. Although none indicated it was the subject of the news article, the Ohio officials "suspected" Honda was the most likely candidate to build a factory in the United States. Duerk explains: "Although Toyota sold the most cars in America of the three companies, that total represented only a small percentage of its worldwide sales. Nissan had the highest percentage of its foreign market in North America, but even that percentage represented a small number compared to Nissan's domestic sales. On the other hand, Honda's North American sales accounted for nearly 50 percent of its total production, so its American operations were much more vital to Honda."

It wasn't until the middle of the following January that Shige Yoshida, a Honda vice-president in California, contacted Duerk. Yoshida asked to meet with Duerk and the governor in Columbus, requesting the meeting be held at a downtown hotel to maintain confidentiality. Cedrick Shimo, a Honda vice-president and a Japanese-born American, accompanied Yoshida to serve as a translator. The two Honda executives arrived on a record-breaking cold day. Yoshida asked Duerk if Ohio was always so cold.

Yoshida asked a lot of questions, jotting the answers on a small pad. Rhodes and Duerk pushed Ohio as the ideal location because of its proximity to a large portion of the U.S. market, its good transportation system, and because it was close to many automobile parts manufacturers. When the meeting adjourned, the Honda executives did not indicate whether Ohio would get the plant. "We didn't know a whole lot more than we did before the meeting," Rhodes tells. "But we did find out that it was Honda who was planning to build in the United States, and the states of Michigan, Indiana, Illinois, and Tennessee also were candidates for the site."

About mid-April, Yoshida was back in Ohio asking more questions. This time Duerk furnished him with a labor study produced by the Ohio Bureau of Employment Services. And once more, state officials were put on hold. The telephone call Duerk had been waiting for came two months later. Yoshida asked to see some sites, so for several days Duerk and a team of Honda representatives toured the state in search of a fifty- to one-hundred-acre parcel of farmland. The group visited fifty to sixty sites, but none were particularly appealing.

Yoshida indicated that Honda needed a site to build a motorcycle factory with room for expansion. "Who knows," he said, "if things go well, perhaps someday we'll manufacture automobiles in this country." With that, the Honda delegation headed back to California.

A few weeks later, a contingent of Honda officials was back

in Ohio to see five more choice locations, flying from site to site in a state-owned airplane.

On a flight from Columbus to Dayton, Yoshida asked if it would be possible to fly over the Transportation Research Center. The TRC, about 50 miles northwest of Columbus, was a 7.5-mile, high-speed auto test track owned and operated by the state of Ohio; it was spread out over 8,000 acres, and was considered one of the best independent testing tracks in the world. Both domestic and foreign automobile companies used the TRC to conduct various tests regarding vehicle dynamics and new model development.

After flying over the testing track twice, Yoshida asked if he could go down and take a look at it, and the small plane landed on a TRC skid pad.

After touring the TRC, the Japanese executives asked dozens of questions about water, zoning, and available industrial land.

The search team was interested in a 260-acre tract of land adjacent to the TRC property, which was six miles west of Marysville, a town of 8,400. Honda officials had wanted a site that would be within an hour's drive of a major airport, and Marysville was that close to both Dayton and Columbus. Two other advantages of the site were that it was located on U.S. Route 33, and it backed up to railroad tracks.

When the Honda executives returned that summer to work out the details of a final contract, the state of Ohio agreed to provide $2.5 million in direct aid, primarily to improve roads and utilities. Honda acted quickly, buying the entire tract with options to buy several hundred more acres from the landowner and from the state-owned TRC.

Honda signed a formal agreement with the state on October 11, 1977 for Honda to begin Phase I, which entailed building and operating a motorcycle plant. The motorcycle plant was incorporated as Honda of America Manufacturing (HAM).

A significant attraction of the Ohio location was the type of people who lived in the surrounding rural area. Upon visiting several manufacturing plants in the midwest, Honda officials were convinced that the local residents possessed a similar work ethic to those Japanese who lived in rural areas near the company's large and successful plant in Suzuka. Honda believed high-quality products could be produced by the local Ohio work force.

Yet at the time, many felt Honda would fail in Ohio because Americans could not produce the same quality workmanship as the Japanese. In fact, when Honda announced its plans to build the plant, some of the most formidable objectors were Honda motorcycle dealers. Dealers across the country urged the company to continue manufacturing its products in Japan. Their concern, of course, was that inferior made-in-America motorcycles could ruin their businesses.

THE OPENING OF HAM

Once the decision to build in Ohio was made, Honda acted quickly. Negotiations with local contractors were completed and construction soon was underway. By mid-1978, while the plant was being built, six Japanese employees relocated to Ohio and leased a temporary 2,000-square-foot office in a suburban Columbus building.

Japanese managers devoted a major portion of their time recruiting the first American workers who would assemble the first HAM motorcycles. All of the managers pitched in to help with the recruiting effort, including Shige Yoshida, who primarily had a purchasing background. Now his duties also included administration, accounting, and production control. The three key recruiters were Kazuo Nakagawa, then president of HAM, Shige Yoshida, and Dan Minor, an attorney on loan from a leading Columbus law firm that represented Honda. Predictably, the recruiting chores were the most tedious and time-consuming the men encountered. HAM had received 3,000 job applications by the time the company had hired its first 100 *associates,* a term HAM applies to all employees.

In the beginning, recruiting the key people was the top priority. These hand-picked individuals would serve as the nucleus that later would be expanded into a large work force. It was essential to pick the right people from the start—and build with them. So, unlike the typical short interviews conducted by domestic auto makers hiring production workers, HAM applicants were interviewed extensively. The first interview generally lasted an hour, and good candidates were interviewed twice more, often by two or three top managers. Because some of the applicants worked during the day, the Honda recruiting team conducted interviews during the evenings and on Saturdays.

The first American hired permanently was Al Kinzer, now HAM's vice-president and engine plant manager. Like many others who came aboard during the early days of HAM, he was attracted by the opportunity to participate in the start of a new manufacturing operation. And he, like most of the recruits, had been a motorcycle enthusiast. One thing in particular attracted his attention during the interview; he recalls thinking, "If HAM can meet its initial objective of producing high-quality motorcycles, the company can pursue the idea of producing automobiles here." With an in-depth background in personnel and industrial relations, Kinzer soon found himself working long hours conducting extensive interviews to hire others for the soon-to-be-opened motorcycle plant.

HAM officials decided to hire people who lived within a thirty-mile radius of the plant. All of these men and women would be gleaned from the small towns and farming areas in rural central Ohio. This plan coincided with the company's commitment to support the local communities.

DEVELOPING A CORPORATE CULTURE

From the beginning, Honda didn't intend to duplicate the management system of its Japanese plants, nor did it want to pattern itself after an existing American organization. And so it followed that HAM's first priority was to establish its own set of policies and procedures.

To accomplish this, the newly transferred Japanese managers and the first-hired American managers began the difficult task of developing a new corporate culture, starting with the basics, one at a time.

The newly formed management team spent hours covering topics ranging from how to produce the first payroll check to what, if any, insurance benefits should be provided. The list went on and on. Discussions included every conceivable consideration for a new company. The managers even spent hours discussing what to call the people who worked at HAM. During a discussion of how the organization should be structured, the group debated what titles to give men and women in supervisory positions. Should a first-line manager, for example, be called a supervisor, foreman, superintendent, or production coordinator? The latter finally was selected. Next the group decided that no one would be referred to as a worker or an employee. Instead, each individual would be called an associate because the term described how each person would relate to the other members of the organization. It also reflected a feeling of respect for the individual, compared to a title that implied a subordinate role.

During one of these sessions, the discussion became heated over the issue of wearing uniforms like Honda's Japanese employees. The debate focused on whether people would think the new plant was trying to make associates appear too "Japanese." Some expected associates to resist wearing a standardized uniform. Then the managers hotly debated the need to have locker rooms for associates to change into and out of their uniforms. The Americans insisted that the associates never would need a locker room because they would wear their uniforms to and from work. The Japanese managers said locker rooms were essential and everyone would use them. The locker rooms were installed, but as it turned out, about half of HAM associates wear their uniforms home.

Al Kinzer recalls how the group spent several hours talking about what kind of lunchroom the plant should have. "We covered everything from vending machines to a staffed cafeteria," he tells. "Then, in the middle of the discussion, someone said, 'Wait a minute, here. Why are we starting this debate at this point? We first should discuss the issue of whether we even should have a room designated for eating meals. Isn't this the basic question we should be addressing?'"

Kinzer points out that the lunchroom discussion epitomizes the approach taken on all subjects. Nothing was assumed. "Too often," Kinzer states, "a person will come to a meeting with a preconceived idea based on his or her experiences. For instance, where does it say a company has to have a place for people to eat? Well, we started with the assumption that there doesn't have to be such a place, and from there we debated. Of course, in the end, we concluded that HAM would have a cafeteria, but my point is that nothing was assumed.

"We discussed everything: morning warm-up exercises, open offices, nonsmoking areas, shift rotations, and overtime. So we labored for what seemed like endless hours over the most minute points; as a result, I think we ended up with something that's unique."

Just as the discussion about wearing uniforms became heated, so did the morning warm-up exercises stir quite a debate. Here too, there was some opposition because it was also believed that people would interpret it as too "Japanese." In the Marysville area, it would indeed mark a first. However, conducting brief limbering up exercises prior to the beginning of each shift was believed to help reduce stiffness, which, in turn, would decrease possible injuries, so an affirmative decision was reached. In the beginning, associates didn't take the warm-up sessions seriously, but as time passed, a growing number participated in the daily ritual, even though it is not mandatory to do so.

Production was set to begin September 9, 1979, and HAM's management realized that associates needed to learn how to meet Honda's high standards. After all, most of the associates had never even worked in a manufacturing plant. But Honda had anticipated an inexperienced labor force; no motorcycle plants were operating anywhere in Ohio, so it was not possible to hire experienced workers. And Honda didn't work that way, anyway. It preferred to develop its own people because doing so reduced the chances of people bringing bad work habits with them. For this reason, an associate with painting experience would sometimes be put in the welding department. Honda wanted to teach specific skills so associates would strive to meet or surpass the company's standards. Like the plant itself, everyone would begin with a fresh start.

Among the first hired was a small group of twelve associates who had some manufacturing experience, including a foreman who had worked for a nearby motor home manufacturer, a welder, and a former machinery plant manager who was brought aboard as production manager. As a matter of interest, all of the original twelve men still work for Honda, and all have advanced to managerial positions.

Each new associate received good old-fashioned on-the-job training. Most of the Japanese associates had worked as engineers at the company's large motorcycle factories in Japan. These transferees worked tediously with the newly hired associates, teaching the basic techniques of motorcycle production. They spoke little English, so visual aids were used whenever possible. The training concentrated on demonstrations, followed by each trainee doing what he or she had watched the manager do. The emphasis always was on quality. The new workers were always given a reason why, not simply an order to "do it." While the Japanese engineers were hard taskmasters, they were exceptionally patient, always encouraging individual participation and questions.

The first team of associates to actually assemble motorcycles was a group of sixteen who were supervised by five Japanese engineers. During their first two weeks, their training was limited to the proper use of tools. This was followed by another two-week period of assembling and disassembling ten models each day. This routine was repeated again and again. Each team member was taught every process until each was capable of doing any other associate's job. Following these two weeks, everyone received a specific job assignment. In the meantime, a valuable lesson had been learned that would apply every day at Honda: *teamwork*.

Shortly after they were hired, many of the new associates were dispatched to Honda plants in Japan where they learned how to weld, paint, and assemble motorcycles according to exact specifications. They received extensive briefings before they left Ohio; after all, it was a big risk for the employer to send them halfway around the world and back, and a big responsibility for the associates. Shige Yoshida smiles as he recalls a two-hour briefing when, during a question-and-answer session, someone asked, "How do I get to the Columbus airport?" As it turned out, this was the first trip the associate had ever taken on an airplane.

In Japan, the American associates witnessed each process from start to finish, from raw materials and parts to pipe bending, welding, painting, and finally, assembling the finished product. During these visits, which lasted from two to six weeks, the associates were exposed to the Honda philosophy. Honda made a large investment in each new associate, and the company apparently received its money's worth because the associates' quality of work vastly improved after they returned. Honda officials explain: "In addition to our large investment in production equipment, we believe in putting our money into people. Yes, it is expensive, but we never hesitated to spend the money. After all, Honda plans to be in America for a long time, so we didn't worry about the short-term costs."

On September 10, 1979, sixty-four associates showed up for work at the 260,000-square-foot plant on the first day of production. Ten dirt bikes were assembled that day.

TAKING THE BIG STEP—AUTOMOBILE PRODUCTION IN THE UNITED STATES

The daily production of ten dirt bikes (model CR250) was just the beginning. Once HAM was satisfied with the quality of these first units, the numbers began to increase. By the end of its first twelve months, HAM was producing the CR250 and CBX street bike model at an annual rate of 24,000 units. During the early part of 1980, the quality of HAM's motorcycle production had reached the point that Honda began thinking seriously about entering Phase II at HAM—producing automobiles. This was a much bigger and more daring step because an auto plant costs many times more than a motorcycle plant. It also meant competing with the "Big Three."

Honda Motor Company president Kiyoshi Kawashima had his share of sleepless nights. Several feasibility studies had been completed, and each showed that a U.S. auto plant would operate at a loss. The CEO let it be known that if a simple, binary yes/no decision was presented, he would vote no. But Kawashima used a philosophy that allowed four decisions:

> Yes
> No, and yet yes
> Neither yes nor no
> No

Tetsuo Chino, general manager of American Honda at the time, confesses that he "dressed up the figures just a bit" because the marketing organization wanted a made-in-the-U.S.A. car to sell. Kawashima spent hours listening to the pros and cons of the study, which produced a "no, and yet yes" answer. This answer made his decision difficult because there was no clear-cut recommendation to take what was deemed a major risk. Even so, he announced, "Go ahead anyway," with what he knew would be the company's largest undertaking by far outside of Japan. Again, the company decided to proceed partially because of its commitment to manufacturing its products in the markets it serves. The decision also coincided with the company's belief that it must face its toughest challenges first.

In December 1980, ground was broken for a 1-million-square-foot, $250-million automobile plant. On November 1, 1982, production of the first Accord began. The plant was expanded to 2.2 million square feet in 1986, and Honda then began making Civics that July on a second production line. Upon its completion, HAM became America's most integrated automobile plant, housing stamping, welding, painting, plastic injection molding, assembly, and quality assurance operations under one roof.

A COMMITMENT TO AMERICA

At the time of this writing, Honda's U.S. investment totals about $1.7 billion. One of Honda's long-term goals is to have its U.S. operations become an integrated, self-reliant, domestic unit. By the early 1990s, Honda's North American operations will have the capability to completely design, engineer, and build a car, although certainly much technical know-how will be shared by Honda in Japan. U.S. labor and parts accounted for about 60 percent of the content of Honda's 360,000 American-built 1988 automobiles, and that figure is expected to increase to 75 percent by 1991.

To reach these numbers, HAM built a 235,000-square-foot engine plant in Anna, Ohio, a town fifty miles west of the Marysville operations. The Anna plant began producing motorcycle engines on June 20, 1985, and like the original motorcycle factory, it too started on a small scale. In May, just before its official opening, its preproduction (trial production) volume was set at ten to twenty engines daily. Associates built the engines, took them apart, and rebuilt them, again and again, until satisfied that the quality met Honda's high standards. The first engines were built for the Gold Wing motorcycle. Soon afterward, Honda approved plans to build Civic automobile engines, which went into production in September 1986. Aluminum wheel production began in January 1987. By 1991, the Anna plant will build Accord engines, as well as automobile transmissions, drive train components, suspension components, brakes, and forged parts.

A constant corporate goal is to establish Honda in the United States as an American corporation. As Tetsuo Chino says, "Americanization of production is part of that. We are increasing our R&D in this country to assure that our cars are accepted by the American people. Most of the profits made in this country are reinvested here. Last, we want to Americanize management. Ultimately, we would like to see Honda accepted as an American company."

AND STILL MORE HONDA MANUFACTURING

Some people who work at Honda say it is neither an automobile *nor* a motorcycle company. "We are an engine company," they insist.

In Swepsonville, North Carolina, a hundred or so associates who work for the Honda Power Equipment (HPE) plant are apt to agree. The plant manufactures lawn mowers and general-purpose engines. HPE opened its doors in the spring of 1984, again in line with the philosophy of manufacturing products in those markets it serves. North Carolina was chosen because the southeastern portion of the United States was the company's largest market. Second, a high percentage of the lawn equipment industry's suppliers are located in the area. HPE also has a policy of selling made-in-the-U.S.A. products made with American parts. Although a different product line is produced in the North Carolina plant, the same basic Honda management principles are followed.

In November 1986, Honda opened another North American automobile plant, this time in Alliston, Ontario, a small community about sixty miles north of Toronto. It's probably more than coincidence that the work force in this rural Ontario community resembles the Marysville area. As HAM serves the United States, this factory was built to serve the Canadian market. A marked difference was, however, that the Ohio plant had experienced Honda motorcycle associates before it began to assemble automobiles. In Canada, the newly hired associates were developed from scratch to build automobiles. The same pattern was repeated: Canadian associates were sent to Japan; Japanese engineers were sent to Canada. Of course, many associates and engineers were sent to and from the Ohio plant. Just as the Sayama plant in Japan had been HAM's "sister" company, the U.S. automobile plant plays a similar role to the Canadian affiliate.

At present, Honda plans to assemble 80,000 automobiles at the Alliston plant by 1989 with an estimated 700 associates. And like the friendly competition that exists between HAM and the Honda plants in Japan, the Canadian operation strives to build automobiles with the same or better quality than those made in the United States.

II

A Customer-driven Company

4

The American Marketing Organization

BY THE EARLY 1990s, Honda plans to produce more than 500,000 cars in the United States and another 80,000 in Canada. Add to this the company's current 420,000 U.S. imports, and sales total 1 million units. This equals about 50 percent of Honda's projected worldwide sales. Its 1987, U.S. sales of 738,000 cars exceeded the number sold in Japan.

Back in 1974, when Honda boldly decided to become the first Japanese company to manufacture automobiles in the United States, top management knew the risks, but they also knew the upside: the U.S. market's enormous potential. Toyota and Nissan dominated the fiercely competitive and overcrowded Japanese automobile industry, so Honda recognized that its homeland was a limited-growth market. If the company wanted to enter the elite ranks of world-class auto makers, it had to seek markets outside of Japan.

A few years ago when the forty largest Honda auto dealers came from Japan to tour HAM, it was inevitable that they would want to visit a few dealerships. These visits turned out to be a staggering experience. Instead of one- and two-car dealerships, these dealers gazed in astonishment at American dealerships, landscaped with acres of parked cars converging on massive showrooms and repair shops.

The dealers' amazement emphasizes how American marketing differs vastly from that of Japan. Honda could not rely solely on its Japanese marketing know-how to succeed in the United States. What worked in Japan had little application in the United States. Opportunity? Yes. But Honda executives knew they had to get it right the first time—they could not afford big mistakes.

MOTORCYCLE MARKETING STRATEGIES

Honda is the world's leading motorcycle manufacturer, holding more than a 50 percent share of the world market. While Honda outsells all of its motorcycle competition combined, it still concentrates on expanding its market. John Petas, senior vice-president of the U.S. motorcycle division, says: "As the leader in our industry, we want not only to continue being number one but we also want a bigger market. Numbers two and three will continue trying to beat us, so we must remain innovative to stay on top. We must never become complacent or satisfied."

To stay in front, Honda consistently dominates the motorcycle racing circuit. In 1986, for example, Honda became the first company to win ten major U.S. race championships. In Daytona, for example, an incredible thing happened. *The first fourteen racers to cross the finish line were riding the company's new Hurricane 600 model.* What this tells the consumer is clear.

The Honda motorcycle division is by no means a niche marketing organization. Honda's myriad products, from small $400 scooters to the top-of-the-line luxury touring motorcycle, the 1,500-cc six-cylinder Gold Wing, all get high marks.

While the typical motorcycle enthusiast probably has a mechanical background and thus prefers to do his or her own repairs, the average scooter buyer has no such inclination. When Honda decided to expand the scooter market by appealing to buyers who wanted an inexpensive product, it had to pursue a brand new, untapped market. Honda had to appeal to people who wanted a quick ride to the supermarket, who needed only to travel back and forth to school, or who just liked riding a scooter. After honing its advertising campaign to reach this new market, Honda's scooter sales from 1983 through 1985 exceeded what the entire U.S. industry had sold during the past twenty years!

Honda's offbeat motorcycle ads have become a trademark for American Honda's scooters, and the company credits its advertising campaign with resuscitating what had been a weak motor scooter market for several years in the United States. Through provocative advertising, the company "appeals to people who have a youthful attitude and try to be different," says an advertising manager for Honda scooters. "That means young people, but it also includes the young at heart" (i.e., the middle-aged lawyer who would show up at court on a scooter).

One television commercial, for example, has the camera zooming in for a close-up of the scooter as an announcer growls, "If you have an itch, scratch it." Translation: Many people fantasize about riding a scooter, so they should act on this dream. "Now that people know scooters aren't funny little toys," the manager adds, "we need to make them more accessible by illustrating the exhilaration of riding one."

As mentioned earlier, Honda began selling the small N600 automobile in the United States mainly as a secondary product in domestic dealerships' foreign car departments. At first, sales were slow. But after introducing the Civic with the CVCC engine, the American consumer suddenly looked at Honda with renewed respect. With revived momentum, the company was able to establish a network of its own independent dealerships.

Every beginning business student knows that to successfully market any product, there must be an avenue through which a manufacturer can reach the customer. Without adequate distribution, even the finest product is doomed to fail. In the U.S. automobile industry, a manufacturing firm relies on its network of independent dealerships as its source of distribution.

In Japan, Honda's late entry into the automobile business made it virtually impossible to find good locations. Years earlier, Toyota and Nissan had established vast dealership networks throughout the country. Consequently, Honda's growth in its native land was limited from the start because prime real estate and open territories simply were not available. This was not the case in the United States. Despite the number of car lots blanketing the American countryside, plenty of space remained.

Honda first introduced its cars in the United States by distributing them through other auto makers' dealers, but once its products were accepted by the public, the company's game plan was to seek experienced dealers who knew the business inside and out—car merchants who knew how to run a profitable business and understood how to treat customers properly.

Honda had to persuade the American public that the Honda car reflected high quality at a reasonable price. Once the Honda was perceived as such, the company easily attracted experienced, well-connected dealers. It had, indeed, built a better mousetrap. Honda's first automotive mousetrap was its CVCC engine, and when *Reader's Digest* featured an article titled, "From Japan—A 'Clean Car' That Saves Gas" in its December 1975 issue, the name Honda suddenly took on new meaning in the United States. The five-page article gave a detailed explanation of how Honda's technological breakthroughs had produced a superior engine that not only minimized carbon monoxide, hydrocarbons, and nitrogen oxide but increased fuel efficiency as well. In part, the article stated:

> Late in 1972 Honda shipped three cars equipped with its new CVCC engines (Honda's trademark for its new engine) to the Ann Arbor, Mich. Emission Testing Laboratories of the U.S. Environmental Protection Agency. There, without catalytic converters or other add-ons, every car far surpassed the tight emission standards scheduled to go into effect by 1975. The federal standards, for example, prescribed hydrocarbon emissions no greater than .41 grams per mile. But, even after running 50,000 miles on the test dynamometer, the CVCC engines were emitting .24 grams of hydrocarbon per mile. Against the federal 1975 carbon-monoxide

limit of 3.4 grams per mile, Honda engines averaged only 1.75 grams. And, compared with the federal nitrogen-oxide-emission ceiling of 3.1 grams per mile, the Honda averaged .65 grams of these smog-producing gases.

Then came another surprise. Honda engineers installed their stratified-charge cylinder head and carburetor on the eight-cylinder engine of a 1973 Chevrolet Impala. When the Environmental Protection Agency tested this big-engine, full-size car, it found that Honda's modifications had reduced emissions substantially below the 1975 federal limits and that fuel economy was increased.

Meanwhile, after the Japanese government had carried out its own tests on a fleet of Honda CVCCs and found that their emissions were safely below the newly enacted Japanese limits, which are even stricter than those in the United States, Honda began mass production. About a year ago it placed a small, four-door model powered by the CVCC engine on sale in Japan. Since then, thousands of Japanese motorists have driven it for millions of miles, getting as much as 40 miles per gallon of gas. Now, with production stepped up to about 360,000 cars a year, Honda has begun exporting CVCC sedans and hatchbacks to its U.S. dealers.

The article went on to mention that while the new engine added about $170 to the cost of a conventional internal-combustion engine, it eliminated the need for catalytic converters and other add-ons costing about $350, providing a net savings of $180. "And this savings is increased by every mile the car is driven because of the new engine's fuel economy," the article revealed.

Honda's marketing staff wasted little time getting the word out to automobile dealers across the country, mailing out tens of thousands of copies of the story. The *Reader's Digest* was just one of many articles that acclaimed Honda's breakthrough technology—many of the automobile industry's most prestigious publications also raved about the CVCC. Almost overnight, Honda had earned credibility. Owning a Honda dealership suddenly became a sound business opportunity, and the positive publicity helped Honda win over many successful dealerships.

The company solicited only those dealers who knew how to operate a successful car business. "When you take on a dealer who has done a good job with one of the 'Big Three,' the guy is going to make it with us, too," says Senior Vice-President Jack Billmyer, who heads National Auto Field Sales. "Picking the right dealer can help you avoid a lot of problems down the road. If he's been operating a Ford franchise for the past ten years, he's gone through both the bad times and the good. If the guy is still around, the thing that's kept him in business is his knowledge of how to take care of his customers. That's the kind of dealer we want."

Billmyer explains that signing up the most desirable dealer in an area takes a great deal of persistence and patience. He recalls an experience back in the early 1970s with one particular dealer who owned a prosperous Oldsmobile franchise in a southern city. "The dealer was selling about 200 cars a month and had an excellent location. When I first phoned him, he said he was considering another import and didn't even know what a Honda looked like. So I drove one out to his place to show him. He is at least six feet three and the first thing he told me was, 'Gee, this car looks awfully small.'

" 'Well, I drove it out here, and I'm as tall as you are,' I answered. 'Come on, get in and drive it.'

"The dealer invited his general manager and sales manager, both big men, to join him for a ride. When they came back, they all had smiles on their faces and asked me some pertinent questions. After a few hours, the dealer told me to contact him in a couple of weeks for his answer. In the meantime, I had ten other dealers in the area who would have signed up that day, but he was the one I wanted. So I waited, and we got him. He built a Honda dealership right next to his Oldsmobile franchise, and recently, he opened a second exclusive dealership with us. As we expected, he's done a great job, and I never regretted waiting for his response."

While today the company wants to attain the highest market share possible of the U.S. automobile market, its initial ambition was just to sell its American inventory. Even before voluntary restraints went into effect in 1981, Honda could not provide a sufficient number of automobiles in the United States because the company's production in Japan had always operated at full capacity. Because demand was increasing steadily each year, dealers always had waiting lists of customers who wanted to buy Hondas.

The Voluntary Restraint Agreement that Japan adopted in 1981 was supposed to be temporary because the United States was in the midst of a recession and its domestic auto makers needed time to make huge investments and update their model lines. Interestingly, the restraints have been extended every year since, even though the Big Three automakers have been posting near-record profits.

In 1974, Honda sold 43,000 cars in the United States. American Honda had surveyed its dealers and had estimated a tremendous demand for its 1975 models. Dealers had a single complaint: "I'd sell more if you'd just give me more."

Two of American Honda's top marketing executives, Yoshihide Munekuni and Cliff Schmillen, made their annual trip to Tokyo to report on the number of 1975 models to be produced for the American market, and at lunch someone asked them: "How many cars do you want for next year?"

Schmillen looked at Munekuni and said, "Well, if they want to know, I guess we should tell them." He then looked at the top Honda executives gathered at the table and said, "We want 150,000 cars."

There was a lingering silence. The leap from 43,000 to 150,000 had stunned the headquarters executives, who had expected the request to be near 59,000.

While Honda's factory couldn't produce 150,000 cars for the United States, it did manage to roll out 103,000, all of which were sold. As Schmillen later explained, "I'm sure we could have sold the entire 150,000 if we'd had them. In fact, there's never been a year when we overestimated what we could sell in the United States. We've always had the problem of having too few. But that's the kind of problem you want."

Because of Honda's high respect for its American marketing organization, it never tried to call the shots, a common blunder of many foreign companies that market products in the United States. Honda's trust saturated its organization, trickling down to the American marketing organization's faith in its dealers.

Today, its American dealers praise Honda highly because the company gives them so much freedom to run their own businesses. As Schmillen explains, "We were able to attract successful dealers, so we avoid overcrowding them. We always keep our dealers' problems in mind, and we understand that *they've got to make money.* If they're not successful, *we* go down the tubes with them."

Billmyer agrees that Honda is different from other manufacturers because "we don't tell our dealers how to run their businesses. We have too much respect for them. Of course, when you work with professional dealers, it's not necessary to hold a tight rein on them."

To support its dealers, Honda established ten zone offices across the country run by managers with hands-on experience. "Whenever possible, we try to hire people who have worked in the retail end of the business," Billmyer emphasizes. "I can teach the wholesale business to our field reps, but I don't want anyone who never sold a car out there telling our dealers how to do it."

This approach has produced excellent results. In 1987, *Ward's Auto World,* a respected automotive publication, asked readers: "If you had to start over, what franchise would you like to have?" Honda was overwhelmingly the first choice. No wonder. Honda dealerships have the highest average unit sales, the lowest inventories, and are the most profitable.

CATERING TO THE MARKETPLACE

In part, Honda's marketing success in the United States can be attributed to a philosophy of "when in Rome, do as the Romans do." This does not, however, imply that the company follows the lead of other automobile companies. Honda *listens* to its customers and then builds the cars those customers want, producing cars that suit the American consumers' tastes.

A U.S. Honda design team, stalemated on a trunk design project, spent an afternoon in a Disneyland parking lot observing what people put into and took out of their car trunks and what kind of motion was involved. It was a classic example of on-the-spot research. Honda didn't hire an outside market research firm to provide stacks of data about trunk usage, but took a more direct approach and ultimately came up with a new design.

An Accord owner tells, "On weekends, I use my car as a pickup truck. Obviously a sedan isn't supposed to carry lumber, but by folding down my back seat I can place boards through the trunk. I used to think I was the only person who used my Accord that way, but then I talked to other owners who do, too."

Unlike many auto makers that depend strictly on design engineers to develop cars, Honda relies on a program called Sales, Engineering, Design (SED). It generally takes three to four years for the company to develop a new car, about half the time it takes other automobile companies, and people from sales, engineering, and R&D meet regularly from beginning to end. This leads to a steady flow of ideas from which Honda can *build the cars the customers want.*

Cliff Schmillen, executive vice-president of Honda North America, explains, "The secret of our developing a new model is that people from all divisions *talk to each other.* It sounds so simple, and it is, but this is not common in the automobile industry." Schmillen, who has been in the selling end of the business throughout his career, adds, "Honda salespeople and engineers have a strong mutual respect for one another. The Honda Motor Company has had only three presidents, and each has had an engineering background. I suspect this is the way it's going to be for quite some time, and that's fine with the marketing and salespeople. You see, we're basically an engineering company, and we're all proud of this fact. When you get right down to it, product is everything in this company, so while the engineering people don't interfere with how we sell the cars, they do pay close attention to our suggestions on car trends and styling. And before anything is finalized, they always listen to our feedback."

Honda is constantly seeking feedback from its dealers. Every U.S. dealer has access to the top marketing executives. Even more important, the dealers feel comfortable calling the executives. All top officers call on dealerships, constantly seeking feedback from "the people who are closest to the Honda customer."

Honda engineers and manufacturing managers also travel the country to listen to dealers' opinions. They ask the dealers, "What do you need?" "What about this?" "Do you think this will help you sell more cars?" In Japan, every engineering and manufacturing manager, as part of his or her training, is required to spend six months working at a dealership to develop a clear understanding of customer needs.

While other auto makers boast of listening to consumers and dealers, emphasize quality, and claim they treat their employees with respect, Honda North America President Chino says the proof is in the action.

> When we [Honda] introduced the second-generation Prelude, we didn't put power steering in it. Women drivers complained the steering was too heavy, and within six months' time we put in power steering. We react fast that way.

Fast reaction. That's part of the Honda legend. Contrast this with the story that a GM executive told *Forbes* a while back. When he wanted a pinstripe put on his California-bound cars, production said it would take a year to get it. A pinstripe.

This search for feedback continues through development and sales. For example, when the first newly designed 1982 Accords were shipped to the United States in September 1981, Honda people at the port of delivery reported several problems. Yoshihide Munekuni, now president of American Honda, was down at the docks examining the new models and taking Polaroid photographs of damage incurred during ocean transit. He put his photos in an album and handwrote detailed explanations on the margins. Munekuni then personally delivered the album to Honda's headquarters in Tokyo.

QUALITY IS THE NUMBER ONE
PRODUCT

When asked to describe the company, one dealer simply said, "Honda always is trying to create a better product. They keep striving for perfection."

Another dealer commented, "I am proud to be a Honda dealer. It's a good feeling to have a car I can sell to a friend and not have to make excuses. I've sold some cars I was embarrassed to sell to my customers. Look at the history of diesel cars in this country. I pity the poor dealer who had to sell diesels to his customers. He has to be thinking, 'I'm sorry you got stuck, but there's nothing I can do about it.' He can't afford to buy all of those cars back. And the factory isn't about to do it, either."

Before entering the U.S. market, Honda extensively studied Volkswagen, who had been the largest car importer during the 1950s and 1960s, to find out why the German manufacturer lost its lead. In 1978, it was Volkswagen, too, that became the first foreign auto maker to build cars on American soil. While the American public had a love affair with the Beetle, the study revealed that Volkswagen mistakenly introduced the Rabbit before its engineers got all of the bugs out of it. As a result, Rabbit owners were plagued with defects that often couldn't be repaired at Volkswagen shops. The cars had so many problems that even Volkswagen dealers began refusing them as trade-ins. While Volkswagen eventually came out with a better Rabbit, the damage had been done—Americans perceived Volkswagens as having inferior quality and design. In 1984, Volkswagen replaced the Rabbit with the slightly larger and more powerful Golf model, spending about $200 million to retool the assembly line. But the Golf, too, proved unequal to the Japanese challenge in the small-car market, as did the Jetta compacts introduced in 1984.

In November 1987, Volkswagen announced the closing of its New Stanton, Pennsylvania, plant, becoming the first foreign auto maker to abandon its U.S. manufacturing venture. The *Wall Street Journal* wrote:

The move is seen as an early sign of the shakeout among auto plants expected to continue for several years. And for the pioneer auto maker, the departure culminates at least five years of increasing pressure from Japanese competitors and poor U.S. sales some have linked to an image problem that hurt the company's U.S.-produced cars. . . . Khaled Majeed, an analyst with Drexel Burnham Lambert, Inc., said that many Volkswagen buyers believe "the quality of the cars built in Pennsylvania wasn't up to the quality of the cars [built] in Germany."

"We've had three basic selling points since we started marketing Honda cars in the United States," says Tom Elliott, senior vice-president of auto operations. "We sold value, fuel economy, and quality. The strong yen eliminated our price advantage over the domestics, and since the last oil crisis the cost of fuel was no longer a major factor. So over the years, it has boiled down to quality and providing customer satisfaction. We've conducted surveys on this subject, and it's our durability, reliability, and consistency that sells Honda cars. Quality is our one underlying theme. Honda always has emphasized quality with our production in Japan, and in November of 1982 when we started building cars in the United States, the first ones to run off our assembly line were severely scrutinized. Had HAM not produced cars with the same quality as Japan, our good reputation for quality could have been ruined."

According to a 1985 Gallup survey for the American Society for Quality Control, Americans are willing to pay more for quality products of all sorts. For example, consumers will pay about 50 percent more for a better-quality dishwasher, $454 instead of $300; $497 versus $300 for a television set; $868 instead of $500 for a sofa; and twice as much—$47 versus $20 for a pair of shoes. The report also revealed that most consumers would pay about one-third more for a higher-quality car; $13,581 instead of $10,000, for example.

THE ACURA!

When Honda entered the luxury automobile market in 1986 with its Acura line, the occasion marked another first for the company. No other Japanese car manufacturer ever had marketed a second car line through a separate division in this country.

The Acura's introduction captured the attention of the media. *Road & Track* ranked the Acura Legend Coupe as the Best High-Performance Car in the $22,500–$27,500 price range. The magazine said:

> With a perfect reading of the market, Acura translates the best of the German supercoupe into a beautiful, incredibly capable package at half the price. No competition likely until other upper-echelon Japanese lines attempt to follow suit.

The *New York Times* stated:

> It is too early to pronounce the Acura a long-term success, but the early results are promising. Honda is bringing to the task the same kind of do-or-die determination that has made it Japan's largest seller of cars in America. And in its present challenge, Honda can benefit from its strong reputation in America.

Motor Trend said:

> Honda has risen to its currently lofty status in the United States through the commitment to high-quality fit and finish, combined with spirited and fuel-efficient power plants. Until recently, Honda aimed at the traditional Japanese targets—subcompact and compact economy car buyers; but its success in those market segments, along with the monetary pressures of the dollar/yen exchange rates, prompted the Tokyo firm to begin a bold, new venture. Luxury cars bring bigger profits, and Honda felt it could compete with the Europeans in the lucrative high-content, performance market. Thus the Acura was born.

The *Columbus Dispatch* made this reference to Honda:

> A trendsetter in the U.S. market. It was the first Japanese auto maker to build a factory in the United States and the first to set up a separate dealer network to sell an upscale line of cars, the Acura line.

Elliott explained why Honda set up a separate network of dealerships. "We felt that Honda can't be all things to all people. The potential buyer of a deluxe car such as a Mercedes-Benz feels uneasy about making an expensive purchase from a company that also makes an $7,000 car. When you think about cars in the class of a Mercedes or a BMW, the name Honda doesn't spring to mind because we've created an image that our products stand for lower-priced fuel economy, a good value for your money and, of course, quality. While these are wonderful attributes, they don't gel with a high-price image. So rather than trying to have Honda simultaneously cater to both markets, we established a brand new image for our Acura line—one that projects luxury and performance. For this reason, we've positioned Honda and Acura at opposite ends of the spectrum."

Honda feared some luxury-car buyers would snicker at the thought of plunking down $19,000 for a Honda. The Honda name, therefore, won't appear on either the Legend or the Acura's other model, the lower-priced Integra (except on the engine's valve covers and in the small print inside the door frame).

"Honda's not dumb," says Leon Mandel, editor-in-chief of *AutoWeek*. "If Honda wants to sell a car to a different segment of buyers, it must disassociate itself from the rather utilitarian image of its line of Hondas."

"At the same time, Honda owners know that we make the Acura, just like the public knows Ford makes Continentals," Elliott points out. "We have customers who bought the N600 back in 1970 and later purchased the Civic in the mid-1970s. In the late seventies, many of these same customers became Accord owners. Now if a company wants people to stay with its products over a long period of time, it must have something to offer its customers as they get older and become more affluent. We feel we can keep these customers by offering them our Legend and Acura automobiles as an alternative to the Mercedes or BMW."

So far, the Acura buyers are exactly the customers Honda is seeking. A demographics study shows these buyers are well-educated, affluent people who formerly were drawn largely to European imports. The average annual family income of the buyers of a Legend coupe is about $90,000 compared to about $34,000 for the average new-car buyer.

Unlike the company's earlier struggles in setting up its U.S. car and motorcycle distribution, this time there was a strong demand for Acura franchises. With its proven success in the United States, Honda had the luxury of picking its Acura dealers. By the end of 1986, the Acura Division had 50 dealerships, each owned by a successful Honda dealer. Each was a separate Acura dealership and, for the most part, located in another town from where the dealer owned a Honda franchise. Sales in the first year totaled 52,869 units, missing its goal of 55,000. The 1987 sales came in at 109,000, which exceeded the company's goal of 105,000. By 1990, the company wants to sell 220,000 to 250,000 units a year through 600 dealerships. As a comparison, in 1987, 87,839 BMWs and 89,918 Mercedes were sold in the United States.

Once more we witness Japan's youngest major automobile company taking a bold step into the unknown and succeeding beyond anyone's imagination. Honda again displayed its foresight and prompt responses to demand, compared to its seemingly slow-moving Japanese competitors, Toyota and Nissan. Since the Acura, both those auto makers have announced they will enter the luxury car business in the United States, but many experts doubt either company can duplicate Honda's success. Many believe Honda decided to enter the high-priced market because it already had won acceptance with its acclaimed Accord, which sells for about $15,000.

The ultimate success of the Acura Division rests with the quality of its product. In this respect, the car already is establishing enormous credibility among those who rate automobiles. In its December 1987 issue, *Road & Track* picked the Acura Legend Coupe as one of its 1988 "Ten Best Cars in the World" in both value and passion. The magazine's description of the Acura read like ad copy:

> The new brand name with instant credentials. This able, elegant sedan fully lives up to them with an authoritative, unbeatable

combination of styling, refinement, and a purring powertrain that growls on demand.

J. D. Power and Associates, a leading automotive research company, ranked Acura number one in its Customer Satisfaction Index for all 1987 models. (Honda was listed as number two. The previous 1986 study, which objectively compared customer satisfaction and servicing during the first year of ownership for all makes and models, showed Honda edging out Mercedes-Benz for the first time.)

THE CAR IS THE STAR

While the "You Meet the Nicest People on a Honda" ads did wonders for motorcycle sales, the same advertising strategy was not appropriate for selling automobiles. Interestingly enough, Honda used a different American advertising agency from the beginning to handle its cars instead of Grey, its motorcycle agency. "When the N600 car was first introduced to America in 1970, it lacked personality and had no identification in the automobile field," says Gerry Rubin of Rubin Postaer & Associates, Honda's automobile advertising agency. "In fact, to some, the N600 was viewed as an extension of the motorcycle. It was too small and underpowered."

The original advertising agency failed to position the N600, partly because the agency actually accentuated the perceived problems of size and power. One ad, for example, featured a woman sitting on the N600's fender, making the car look that much smaller.

When the 1974 Civic Sedan was introduced, Honda felt it needed to change agenices. At the time, Rubin was with the Needham Harper Worldwide agency. He recalls how the firm won the Honda account. "We had a long debate about whether our presentation should be done in Japanese or in English, and finally we decided to stick to our native tongue. We felt that because we were pitching a company called American Honda, they were anxious to relate to the U.S. market in a traditional way. So we did our entire presentation in English and purposely made it visual, featuring a film of our people in a variety of work situations. And, of course, they were shown driving Civics. It was our way of introducing ourselves as real people. We won the account."*

With a limited 1974 budget of only $7 million compared to about $90 million today, the Needham Harper ads appeared almost exclusively in print in traditional magazines such as *Newsweek* and *Sports Illustrated*. After reviewing what the agency believed were a series of revolutionary automobile features, Needham Harper sold the Civic 1200 under the line: "What the World Is Coming to." As Rubin explains, "There were several claims, such as front-wheel drive, dual diagonal brakes, McPherson strut suspension, and rack-and-pinion steering that permitted us to say that Honda was what the world was coming to . . . and it worked. Honda sold 43,000 cars that year, and was ranked number twelve among imports for the year. By communicating visually with two-page magazine spreads, we were able to project an image that we were not, after all, a small car. These ads helped us overcome the public's weak perception of a Honda car."

When Honda introduced its CVCC engine in 1975, it was an ad man's dream. The country was in the middle of an oil embargo. Gasoline prices skyrocketed and gasoline was being rationed. Meanwhile, the domestic auto makers had refused to downsize or create fuel-efficient cars. So along comes Honda with a car that doesn't require unleaded gasoline, thus offering a double savings: Not only was regular gasoline less expensive but the Civic got more miles to the gallon! With this information, Needham Harper presented an ad to American Honda with a bold headline reading: "Runs on Any Kind of Gas." The ad drove home a strong message and had the potential to sell many cars.

*Rubin Postaer & Associates, originally the Los Angeles office of Needham Harper Worldwide, was named Honda's advertising agency in 1986. As a result of a series of mergers that included Needham Harper Worldwide, the Honda account was given to the newly formed Rubin Postaer & Associates.

"Yes, I like it," the then executive vice-president, Yoshihida Munekuni, told Gerry Rubin, "but we can't use it."

"Why?"

"Because next year, Honda won't be able to make this claim so it would be disrespectful to our customer to make it now," Munekuni replied.

As it turned out, the company changed the engine's carburetor to improve efficiency but it no longer could run on leaded gasoline. While Honda could have sold scores of additional cars with the "Runs on Any Kind of Gas" ads, the company refused to compromise what it believed was "a matter of integrity." "Honda thought it would be exploiting the customer," Rubin explains.

Another time, Rubin recalls, the five-speed Civic was the highest-mileage car in America, and after Munekuni saw the screening of an ad reflecting this point, he shook his head and said, "No, I don't think so."

Again, a stunned Rubin asked, "Why?"

"I'm sorry, but we don't have enough five-speeds in our inventory, so after we run out of them, too many of our customers will be disappointed."

As Rubin explains, "The company's philosophy is to act with integrity. Its advertising is an extension of this philosophy."

Beginning in 1977, Honda used "We Make It Simple" as its signature. The message was that its cars were simple to buy, operate, and service. It also conveyed that Honda truly cared about its customers' small concerns. Unlike the advertising of other auto makers, Honda's is low-key and subtle. No pitchmen pound tables or jump on car roofs nor does a Honda ad ever put down a competitor. According to a national survey of dealership owners and general managers conducted by *Ward's Auto Dealer,* an industry publication, Honda's advertising campaign was rated second only to Ford's "Quality is Job 1" ads. However, Ford dealerships outnumbered Honda agencies by a wide margin that probably gave Ford an advantage in the survey's final tally. The article concluded:

Ford and Honda, with consistent (lasting longer than a year or two) themes, project quality and class and tend to generate the right kind of floor traffic—people who can relate to a vehicle's virtues and who are apt to sign on the dotted line.

The "We Make it Simple" campaign was discontinued in the early 1980s and since then Honda has not used a slogan or signature to advertise its cars. The "Simple" theme was dropped because, with the company's extensive line of products, its message became inappropriate. Furthermore, the decision to no longer use slogans and signatures was based on the belief that "the car is the star" and it speaks for itself.

While many of the company's scooter ads featured flashy celebrities, such as actress Grace Jones and Chicago Bears quarterback Jim McMahon, when it comes to automobile advertising, only the car is the star. In fact, unlike the domestic auto makers that show men dressed in tuxedos and ladies in chiffon dresses in front of five-star restaurants and country estates, Honda ads purposely avoid promoting a certain lifestyle so they won't alienate any potential customers. Nor does a Honda ad actually try to sell the cars. "It's not like we're selling a twenty-five-cent bar of soap or some other inexpensive over-the-counter item," Rubin explains, "where it's up to the commercial to make the sale, then the customer spots it on the shelf, impulsively picks it up, and tosses it into a shopping cart. Buying a car requires careful consideration, so the prime objective of our ads is to stimulate enough interest to induce the prospect to come into a Honda showroom. Then it's up to the salesperson to make the sale."

While Honda's advertising is effective, the company probably spends less on advertising per vehicle than any other major automobile manufacturer. Tom Elliott sums it up. "Our product is so good, it sells itself. Ultimately, the word-of-mouth from satisfied customers generates perhaps as much as 50 percent of our business."

5

Providing Superior Service

MOST PEOPLE believe the only service they get these days is lip service. It's sad that so many companies talk about providing good service, but fail to deliver. It seems they're more interested in increasing new sales volume than in making sure their existing customers are satisfied. Chances are, these companies aren't going to make it in today's customer-driven marketplace.

Few would dispute IBM's reputation as one of the world's truly great corporations. In part, its success is a direct result of three principles that founder Thomas Watson, Sr., declared would dictate the company's every action. On his principle about service, Watson said that he wanted IBM to provide the best service by *any* company, not just of those in his own industry. He felt that IBM should strive to provide the best service in the world. Watson mandated that

> every part of IBM's operation would focus on the customers' requirements. Every employee's job description would somehow be related to IBM's goal of providing customers, prospects, and vendors with the best possible service.

Watson's commitment to service was not an idle promise. IBM continues as a dynamic organization that lives by its principles.

Like IBM, providing outstanding service to its customers is a top priority at Honda. In fact, had the company been unable to provide quality service, it probably would have succumbed to the fierce competition from the 247 other motorcycle companies that were fighting for a piece of the pie Honda was after in 1948. It was a dog-eat-dog industry, and those companies that did not service their customers were unable to survive. Not only did Honda survive, but within the incredibly short span of only a dozen years, Honda became the world's largest motorcycle manufacturer, while only a handful of those original competitors remained in the business.

Japan is purported to be the world's most competitive marketplace, and had Honda been unable to succeed in its homeland, the company never would have had the chance to enter the automobile industry in the United States. In Japan, providing outstanding service is not an option; it is a prerequisite for survival. Companies that fail to provide service are hastily swallowed up by the competition. As Cedrick Shimo, vice-president of Honda International Trading, says, "Contrary to what some people think, the Japanese are not better businesspeople than the Americans. But they are more service-oriented because they must be to survive in the fiercely competitive Japan. Not every Japanese company excels in servicing its customers, but the ones that don't aren't likely to succeed. In any event, only the well-operated Japanese companies—the cream of the crop—come to America. These are Japan's 'first-string' companies. The fourth- and fifth-string teams stay home or go out of business altogether."

Honda became one of those first-string teams and ultimately entered a new and vastly different environment, one dominated by three huge domestic manufacturers that ranked numbers one, two, and six in worldwide automobile sales. In the United States, Honda continued to serve its customers, giving them the same brand of dedication and commitment that its Japanese customers received. Placed in a business climate that has failed to pamper its valued customers, Honda was destined to become a superstar.

BUILDING SERVICE AND QUALITY INTO
THE PRODUCT

At Honda, everyone in the company—from the CEO to the assembly line associate—thinks about the customers' needs. Customer satisfaction is everyone's ultimate goal. "The quality of your work is your job security," Honda constantly reminds its associates.

American Honda's senior vice-president of service, Perry Rutan, explains, "The quality of our cars is at such a high that our customer relations operation can be small compared to that at other auto makers. Some people mistakenly believe the problem with quality production is a labor issue, that the American work force is incapable of producing high-quality products. I disagree. About half of our cars sold in the United States in 1987 were built in this country by American labor, and the quality was just as high as our cars produced in Japan. It's management's attitude and its commitment to quality that makes such a difference."

Former IBM vice-president of marketing Buck Rodgers says,

> Service can't be an afterthought. It must be an important part of the marketing plan, and a serious consideration throughout the development of the product, from its very inception. A new product should never be introduced before service has been thought out and tested.
>
> At IBM, service people live at the development site of a new product. They design the maintenance techniques and deal with such questions as: What training will be required to service the product? What diagnostics can be built into it? What is the appropriate support delivery system? Where should spare parts be stocked? In what quantities?

Like other great customer-driven companies such as the IBMs, Hewlett-Packards, and Kodaks of this world, Honda recognizes the need to build service into the manufacturing of its products, even though doing so frequently carries a steep up-front cost. Some companies are unwilling to spend money to save money, just as some executives resisted energy-conservation measures in the 1970s. But the initial investment in equipment and training is well worth making. Eventually, the savings come from avoiding the need for repairs, for paying off warranties, and for settling liability suits, the costs far exceeding those of a quality program.

While Honda has no such written policy, it is an ingrained attitude shared by all associates. "We have a deep concern about taking good care of our customers," Rutan emphasizes. "While many companies debate over costs versus customer satisfaction, Honda never will conserve at the expense of our customers. Because we're more engineering-prone than other automobile manufacturers, with engineers as our top leaders, our main concern always focuses on what happens to our product once it's in the consumer's hands."

Says a Honda dealer who also owns several domestic franchises, "When customers bring their Hondas in for the 7,500-mile checkup, they say: 'I don't know what you're supposed to do to my car, but *please* don't mess it up. It's running great just the way it is.'

"Now that's a welcome sound to hear from customers. With other car manufacturers, we've had customers come in with what we call 'the laundry list.' It's a pickayunish five-page list with dozens of problems. With a Honda, there isn't a list, and if something is wrong, it's fixable. We get the car fixed, the customer is happy, and quickly back on the road."

Another dealer says, "Honda's quality control for its factory paint has higher standards than the domestic auto makers. This eliminates a lot of grief because a paint defect is the first thing a new-car buyer notices. Other dealers have to give the customer a song and dance, talk him into accepting it as-is.

A NIP-IT-IN-THE-BUD
SERVICE ATTITUDE

"If there's a problem with one of our new models," Rutan says, "it won't go away by itself, so we want to fix it immediately. The sooner we can take care of it, the better off we are."

One way to avoid service problems down the road is to have each dealer conduct a thorough inspection before turning the car over to the customer. As Rutan explains, "Our dealers have so much faith in our cars that we are afraid they will take a routine approach to the predelivery inspection because they rarely find anything wrong. But we strongly advise them to pay careful attention just in case something has escaped our quality control efforts at the factory."

Honda dealers across the country attest to how the company continually requests feedback on anything that possibly could be wrong with one of its new models. "We're always paranoid that there might be a pattern," Cliff Schmillen explains, "so we want to know as soon as possible if there is a problem so we can get it fixed." Consequently, the company conducts new-owner surveys to detect early problems with new models. Additionally, reps are sometimes dispatched to Honda dealerships and even meet with car owners to gather first-hand information. All problems are then entered into a computer and studied so that potential trends can be identified.

AMERICANS REALLY DO VALUE GOOD SERVICE

Consumers increasingly find themselves paying more for service—and liking it less. Frustration over service rivals the public's complaints over poor-quality goods. Hang around your favorite service establishment, and often it's just a matter of time before you see fingernails tap or tempers flare.

Some entire industries are reducing service instead of offering more. Try to get a salesperson to wait on you at a discount retail store. Look at the reduced services offered today by the airline companies. Notice the rapidly increasing number of self-service gasoline stations. The list goes on.

A large segment of the U.S. population is willing to pay extra for exceptional service because it perceives good service as good value. How much more will Americans pay for exceptional service? A lot. Who would have thought that Federal

Express, by guaranteeing overnight delivery, could charge a premium amounting to several hundred percent on mail?

Honda recognizes that Americans value service. As Honda's senior vice-president of auto operations, Tom Elliott, says, "Our research shows that the price of a car is not the most important reason why people buy from a particular dealer—outstanding service is. The average customer will pay more to a dealer with whom he or she has experienced good service in the past. Of course, there is a point where a particular dealer can price himself out of the ballpark, no matter how good the service is."

THE GUYS ON THE TECH LINE

One fast way to find a quick, expert solution to a problem is through Honda's Tech Line. The Tech Line is a bank of skilled technicians who are on call to analyze any problem that a dealership mechanic can't solve. Honda mechanics place as many as 2,000 calls a month to this toll-free nerve center in Gardena, California. Each technician handles about ten to fifteen calls a day; the nature of the calls runs the gamut.

The technician will listen carefully to the problem, then talk the mechanic through it if necessary. All solutions are stored in a computer for future reference, so if a technician doesn't have a quick fix, he or she looks to see if the problem has ever come up before.

For example, a mechanic might call to say, "I'm having trouble with the dome light and I've tried everything, but I can't seem to find the cause of the problem."

Upon feeding the information into the computer, the technician responds, "Bill, have you looked for a grounded screw?"

If nothing shows up on the computer, the technician will look at a board that contains the entire wiring harness of each Honda car to trace the problem.

"It's similar to what they do in the movies when the guy in the control tower talks to a person who's never flown an airplane, and gives instruction on how to safely land," says one auto mechanic who frequently has used the tech line service.

Once a problem and its solution are programmed into the Tech Line computer, a problem that once took hours to correct can be solved in minutes. And that service department saving is passed on to the customer.

Another major advantage of the Tech Line is the quick feedback it provides about problems in newly released models. "It serves as an incredibly early warning signal," Rutan explains. "If we spot a trend, the information is relayed within hours to the factory to make the necessary corrections." Rutan points out that the Tech Line department meets for thirty to forty-five minutes each morning to review all unusual calls from the previous day.

While other auto makers operate hot lines of this nature, they generally are manned by a bank of secretaries. Again Honda spends extra money up front to nip potential problems in the bud, which ultimately saves the company millions of dollars.

A SUSHI BAR COMPANY

Norimoto Otsuka, executive vice-president of Honda R&D North America, uses a sushi bar analogy when he talks about how a company must understand its customers. "The sushi chef stands behind the bar in his white uniform and has the sushi ingredients arranged so his customer can view them. He and the customer communicate openly, and the order is placed. Then the chef selects the best ingredients and prepares the meal according to the customer's request.

"Over a period of years, the chef acquires a lot of experience and comes to know his customers very well. Eventually a customer comes to the sushi bar and the chef understands his tastes and how to prepare the food for him. With this information, the chef can fix something special for his customer immediately upon seeing him enter his business establishment. The customer is pleased and says, 'You knew what I wanted even though I didn't say a word.'

"In a similar way, we establish relationships with our customers, and over a period of time we know their needs. Just like the sushi chef, in the automobile business, we, too, must cater to our customers."

Honda dealers understand that repeat business is the key to building successful dealerships, and only through outstanding service do they gain strong customer loyalty. After all, a satisfied customer may buy many cars over his or her lifetime, so each sale represents additional repeat orders as well as referrals to other potential car buyers.

SERVICE, SERVICE, SERVICE— THE MORE, THE BETTER

"It's a shame, but in almost any field, when you get good service, it's an exception, and you're excited about it," says IBM's Buck Rodgers. "It ought to be the other way around."

Rich Port, a past president of the National Association of Realtors, states, "A successful real estate salesperson will provide so much service that the customer will be ashamed to do business with anyone else."

Computers, real estate, automobiles. It doesn't matter what the product is. Every business is a service business, and it's the companies that think *service, service, service* that are most likely to succeed.

In his book, *Quest for the Best,* Stanley Marcus of Nieman-Marcus fame, says this about service:

> Customers have the perception that service is an indication of interest in them as individuals, not just as robots dispensing money. Service means courtesy, graciousness without obsequiousness, appreciation in the form of recognition of patronage, perhaps just a "thank-you," willingness on the part of the seller to go beyond the call of duty on occasion, remembering to telephone when a wanted size or style arrives in stock. All of these qualities add up to the creation of a state of euphoria, which in turn fosters customer loyalty to hotels, stores, automobile dealers, and every other organization which customers patronize.

In Japan, successful Honda dealers understand what exceptional service is all about. If you bought a car from one of them, you'd probably have to leave the country to get the service to stop. Buying the car would only be the beginning. The dealer would send you and every member of your family birthday cards as well as congratulatory cards for promotions, graduations, weddings, and so forth. And when your car needed service, the dealer would pick it up from your home and bring it back when it was done. The automobile field is so competitive in Japan that this phenomenal service is mandatory. The dealers who don't perform fail.

When Honda came to the United States to sell cars, its people were taught how to service customers. Honda had no intentions of slacking off in its service. This attitude has carried over to its network of dealers—the company simply won't stop emphasizing that dealers must constantly satisfy each and every customer in all areas: sales, service, parts, and used cars. "When this happens," explains Tom Elliott, "a dealer's profits are guaranteed to increase."

Honda believes that the three most important contacts a car owner has with a dealership are: (1) the salesperson who sells the car, (2) the service adviser to whom the customer brings the car for servicing, and (3) the cashier the customer pays when doing business with the dealership.

"We're constantly working with our dealerships so their salespeople know how to deliver a sales presentation properly," Elliott points out. "The salespeople must have the proper amount of product knowledge, and of course we want them to know how to service customers. Servicing the customer includes little things like making sure a 'perfect' delivery follows every sale. This means that the car must be clean, runs properly, contains an owner's manual, and so forth. And many people don't know how to correctly operate a car, so the salesperson must demonstrate how to do so. Then, of course, the service adviser and cashier must extend the same courtesy as the salesperson. After all, the dealer isn't in business to take the customer's money and run. And no dealer wants to have anyone leave with such an impression. So again and again, we stress to our dealers that selling a car is only the beginning. 'Service, service, service,' we keep repeating. 'Give the customer so much service he or she will feel guilty even thinking about doing business with another dealership.' "

As global competition intensifies and companies around the world enter each others' markets, cost and quality differences among all sorts of goods and services are shrinking. The company that coddles customers best has a competitive edge.

Getting maximum customer satisfaction is an ongoing, long-term proposition. As Elliott points out, "To really be successful in the automobile industry, it's essential to provide the kind of service that makes each customer want to come back when it's time to buy another car. After all, when you think about how many automobiles an individual owns throughout his or her lifetime, a single car sale is just the tip of the iceberg. Depending upon one's age, a customer potentially can represent several hundred thousands of dollars in future business. Then too, a repeat customer also is a company's most powerful word-of-mouth advertising. If every lifelong, loyal customer persuades just a single friend or family member to become a lifelong customer, then the amount of future business doubles. And if the new customer brings in somebody else . . ."

When asked about Honda's philosophy on service, dealers across the United States say, "We do whatever is reasonable to satisfy a customer. It's easy to sell a Honda automobile, but if the customer is not satisfied, he or she won't come back to buy a second, third, and fourth car. It's like our commercial that says some families have ten or more Hondas in the family. The only way to get repeat business is to get maximum customer satisfaction."

Superior service cannot be a whim—something that is extended to only a select group of customers. "The customer is always king" must be a continuous theme for every business. Nowhere is this slogan more widespread than in Japan where people refer to the customer as "Kami-sama" or God—and this is how the customer is treated. It's a day-in, day-out, ongoing, never-ending, unremitting, persevering, compassionate type of activity. Honda has carried this reverence for its customer to the United States.

Customers are won over *one at a time,* and accordingly,

each is valued. As Cliff Schmillen says, "When it comes to satisfying a customer, every Honda car owner is important to us. I don't care what business you're in, it takes a lifetime to build a good reputation, and once you do you must work even harder to keep it. Or else you can lose it in a single day."

III

Building with People

6

Respect
for the
Individual

A SLIGHTLY BUILT MAN, looking years younger than the mid-forties, his face clear of lines, walks briskly through the automobile plant to a meeting. Although in a hurry, he takes time to retrieve a piece of paper he notices on the spotless floor. Dressed in a white uniform and a green and white Honda cap, he deposits the litter in a nearby can. The name *Iri* is stitched in red lettering above his right breast pocket.

"Good morning, Mr. Iri," the man hears repeatedly as he walks through the plant.

Called "Mr. Iri" by his associates, Shoichiro Irimajiri is the president of Honda of America Manufacturing, Inc. (HAM).

While the uniform has some built-in safety and quality features (no buttons or belts that might get caught in machinery or scratch the paint finish), its fundamental purpose is to tell everyone, loudly and clearly, that no one is more or less important than anyone else. Everyone from the company president to the most recently hired employee dresses in the same manner and everyone is referred to as an associate. Unlike a military uniform with highly visible insignias to depict rank, nobody at Honda stands out in the crowd or can be readily identified as a superior. This is true of all Honda manufacturing plants worldwide.

AN EGALITARIAN ENVIRONMENT

You can drive through any one of the vast parking lots that surround HAM's huge manufacturing plant, but you will see no private parking spaces. Spaces are available on a first-come, first-serve basis, so a newly hired associate who comes to work early will have a shorter walk to the plant's entrance than the president.

In contrast, according to a manager at HAM, life was much different at his last job. "As the personnel manager of my previous company, one of my responsibilities was to assign spaces in the parking lot of the manufacturing plant. There were ninety-nine reserved spaces arranged according to one's rank, with the most prestigious spot closest to the front door. The plant manager had the number one spot, number two went to the second-in-command, and so on. If somebody quit, retired, or died, the spot immediately was vacated and everyone moved up a spot. Once I inadvertently assigned a vacated spot to a new person, and my phone rang off the wall with complaints."

While designating parking spaces may be a petty matter, the business world unabashedly flaunts such status symbols with shameful regularity. Within the confines of many organizations, status is a reminder that some people are more important than others. The list of such perks is endless: private dining rooms, executive bathrooms, direct phone lines, company cars, offices with corner windows, and so forth.

At HAM, you'll find no private dining rooms. Everyone, from the plant manager to an assembly line associate, eats together in the same cafeteria. Side by side, corporate officers, plant managers, and shop floor workers eat their lunch—with no obvious way to tell who does what. As one associate tells, "My first day on the line, I sat down next to a man who looked familiar. I thought he was one of the newly hired guys like myself who I had met during a group orientation. He asked me all kinds of questions about why I chose to work for Honda, what I did before, and what I thought about my first day. Real friendly, I thought. It wasn't until the end of the meal that I realized he was a vice-president who made a brief speech welcoming us to the company the day before."

Not only do engineers and managers eat side by side with production associates but they work on the plant floor with them most of the day. And it's not just to run new ideas by them; engineers and managers also handle parts and equipment. This is not a factory with managers who refuse to get their hands dirty!

NO IVORY TOWERS

You won't find any top executives or managers isolated from the troops in ivory towers or hiding behind closed doors in their plush, private offices. No one at HAM has a private office. The automobile plant, the motorcycle plant, and the engine plant all have large, open office areas where managers, coordinators, staff, and clerical workers work side by side at plain desks. Dressed in uniforms, it's even hard to identify a secretary unless he or she happens to be planted behind a typewriter or computer. And even that doesn't prove anything. It's not uncommon to see managers typing their own memos and letters.

Large, open office areas aren't unique to HAM. Even at Honda's headquarters in Japan, the company's president and CEO shares a large office with other top executives. This particular room is referred to as the executive board room (not the same as a board of directors room, as we know it, which is nothing more than a lavish conference room). It is very much a "working" room, where discussions take place freely. It's on the tenth floor of a sixteen-floor building. Why not the top floor? "When you're on the tenth floor," says the company president, "it's easier to go up and down because you never have far to travel."

Admittedly, adapting to an open-office atmosphere requires some adjustment for an executive used to working within the confines of his or her own private chamber. Some initially complain about the noise, while others grumble that they need privacy for confidential conversations. (Honda has small conference rooms available for this purpose.) But the overwhelming consensus is that the easy access to each other makes it all worthwhile. Honda associates persistently state, "People become accessible. You simply look across the room to see if someone is at his or her desk; there are no intermediary appointment secretaries to deal with."

Is it distracting? Are people unnecessarily interrupted in an open-office atmosphere? Does respect and equality come at too high a cost? Apparently not, according to the productivity numbers of Honda and other companies that incorporate this partition-free environment.

An associate from the factory floor feels at ease when approaching the administrative area and to Honda this is what really counts. It's one thing for an executive at a large manufacturing plant to tell assembly line workers, "I have an open-door policy and welcome each and every one of you to see me any time," but it's an entirely different story when a typical factory worker decides to take the executive up on it.

PUTTING IT TO A VOTE

About six months after HAM opened, several associates complained that the company's forty-five minute lunch period was too long. With no restaurants nearby, associates finished complete meals in only fifteen to twenty minutes. HAM associates were anxious to reduce unnecessary time spent in the dining area and suggested, "We only need thirty minutes, so reduce our lunch period and cut off fifteen minutes at the end of the day." The suggestion was put to a vote, and the lunch period has been thirty minutes ever since.

Another time, when Christmas and New Year's day fell on a weekend, HAM associates voted which weekdays would be deemed holidays.

When a severe snowstorm closed the plant for several days in 1985, HAM found itself far behind schedule. The associates could either write off the loss or work harder to make up for lost time. Consequently, to meet the demand for orders, associates decided to make a commitment. Hence, in a plantwide vote, associates resolved: "Here is where our production is now and here is where we want it to be a year and a half from now. And here is what we need to do to get there." Associates could choose between adding two hours to each shift or working Saturdays. The vote favored working Saturdays. With two shifts to consider, a second vote was taken to decide between every other Saturday or alternating five consecutive Saturdays. The associates chose to work every other Saturday.

While such voting may not be on earth-shaking issues, that votes are taken has positive effects on overall morale. Associates made a commitment to meet certain production quotas, all subsequently achieved. As a HAM executive vice-president said, "It's our belief that Honda should respect the judgment of our associates."

Honda's egalitarian approach includes a system whereby a fired associate can appeal his or her dismissal to a court of last appeal. The names of six peers from a different shift are chosen from a drum, and those selected must have worked at HAM at least for one year. A senior manager serves as the seventh panel member. At the hearing, panel members listen to the fired associate's plea and ask questions. The vote is secret and ballots are drawn one by one until a majority is reached. Afterward, all ballots are placed in an envelope and shredded. To date, about 20 percent of the associates who have made an appeal have been reinstated as a result of these panels.

REACTIONS TO AN EGALITARIAN ENVIRONMENT

In the beginning there was some debate about how Americans would react to working in an egalitarian system. In particular, what would be the attitudes of people holding managerial positions—people who would trade their pinstripes for white uniforms and green and white caps? Would high-ranking men and women forfeit their plush, private offices, fancy luncheon meetings, and other perks that reflected their success?

Obviously, some individuals would not fit into an environment void of private offices, designated parking spaces, executive dining rooms, and the many other frills that are commonly allocated according to an organization's pecking order in American industry. And the idea of wearing a white uniform in place of a traditional suit would be upsetting to some people. There is no question that executive status symbols are meaningful to individuals. Not everyone can adapt to HAM's egalitarian atmosphere. Yet, for the great majority of those who work at HAM, the adjustment to what is, by American standards, an unusual environment, has not been a significant problem. On the contrary, associates appear to enjoy it.

Senior vice-president and auto plant manager Scott Whitlock, aged forty-four, a Harvard Law School graduate, was a partner in a major law firm in nearby Columbus before joining Honda in early 1985. As a senior partner, he had his own corner office and belonged to several private downtown clubs where he regularly met with clients over lunch. On the surface, his background would make him an unlikely candidate for working in a large automotive factory and donning a white uniform. Yet, as one of HAM's top managers, Whitlock thrives on the opportunity of playing a major role in the early stages of a world-class automobile manufacturing venture.

"We've been operating for only a few years and yet we're the fourth largest auto maker in America today," he explains. "To be part of this organization is an exciting experience. Sure, I enjoyed the trimmings I had practicing law. But that's exactly what they were—*trimmings.* In the whole scheme of things, those perks are unimportant to me." He thinks that, to some degree, an egalitarian atmosphere existed at the law firm too. "The dark suit was the accepted uniform there. We wear white ones here."

A female associate says, "The trade-off with the open office concept is that everyone is approachable, and I can walk up to anyone when I want to discuss something, and anyone can come to me. This is a much more efficient way to work, and when you get right down to it, that's what really counts. And wearing a uniform is also a plus. First, it's more comfortable, and second, I don't have to spend a lot of time each morning figuring out what I'll wear."

Yet another associate, a certified public accountant who recently joined Honda, comments that he likes wearing a uniform because "it's part of the egalitarian atmosphere where everyone comes across at the same level. Some of the partners at the accounting firm tended to be condescending—it's not like that around here."

A manager of information systems also has no regrets about having traded his executive wardrobe for a Honda uniform. "I spend a lot of time in the plant," he explains, "and wearing the same uniform as everyone else makes people feel more receptive in talking to me about their problems. The uniform seems to remove communication barriers and allows me to get right into the thick of things. In the past, I was treated as some snooping data processing person who was walking around the floor asking a lot of questions. Here, I'm just one of the guys and that makes a big difference."

AN ACCENT ON YOUTH

Honda's accent on youthfulness is rare even for a Japanese business. Soichiro Honda believed in having the best and most qualified person do the job—seniority never was a high priority in determining the most capable individual for a top position. Consequently, people are promoted by merit, regardless of age. Similarly, managers at Honda's U.S. operations hold the high positions that might normally take an additional five to ten years to achieve where seniority is stressed. At Honda chronological age is less important than a youthful attitude and spirit.

When the company was first founded, out of necessity, a great deal of responsibility was delegated to young people. Both Honda and Fujisawa desired to maintain their youthful enterprise, recruiting those with high levels of energy and imagination. Honda respected the flexible thinking of young people willing to challenge the established ways. Today young employees are encouraged to speak out: "If juniors don't rebel against their seniors, that means there is no progress," Honda Motor Co. president Tadashi Kume says.

When he retired, Soichiro Honda said,

> One thing I never say is, "Young people nowadays . . ." After all, the same thing was said about me when I was young. The younger generations are naturally more advanced. Although I already have reached the age of having to think of the "landing" of my life, a person gets a better feeling when he is pulling back on the control stick to lift the airplane. What I am trying to do is to help the younger people fly safely. So my message to young people is this: "Have your own purpose in life, hold your control stick tight, and fly high."

Throughout Honda's nearly forty-year history, the company has entrusted young people with considerable responsibilities. In 1981, twenty-seven was the average age of the project team that developed the highly successful City, a car sold in Japan that is slightly smaller than the Civic.

Dr. James Womack, professor at the Massachusetts Institute of Technology and a close observer of the automotive industry, says, "Today, Honda's motivated work force is highly productive. But what will happen when those young twenty-five-year-old associates begin to get older and the company no longer adds large numbers of new recruits each year? It will be interesting to see if Honda can continue to generate the same productivity out of a more mature work force that doesn't have the same level of energy." To date, Honda has seen tremendous expansion and consequently has not had to contend with a no-growth period.

FROM MARYSVILLE TO TOKYO

In the United States, it's often considered a big deal when a new employee at a branch office is brought into the home office for additional training. So imagine working at HAM and being sent from Marysville to Tokyo after only a brief period of employment. Hundreds of new associates were sent to Honda's headquarters and plants in Japan, sometimes within a couple of weeks or months of joining the company. These trips were designed primarily to introduce new people to Honda's technological and managerial methods so they could be implemented at HAM.

Depending on the length of the visits—usually two to six weeks—the cost of the trip could range from $5,000 to $10,000 per person, a significant expense to invest in a new employee. After all, Honda had no guarantee that the new associate would remain on the payroll long enough for the investment to be recouped. Yet the cost of the long and tedious trip was never a major issue in Honda's decision to send associates to Japan. It was just something that had to be done for the new plant to succeed. Whenever the need arose, the trip was made.

Frequently, such a mission entailed a particular assignment. The associate could learn a new stamping process, a welding technique, a paint application. It was the individual's responsibility to learn everything about a specific job during a crash-course program—and bring the knowledge back to HAM to teach others. It was, indeed, a heavy load to put on the shoulders of a new employee. In some cases, if the individual failed to absorb detailed and complicated data, his or her mission would have been deemed a failure. But there were no failures—each associate brought back everything his or her assignment had included.

In May 1979, a current manager was hired to work on HAM's soon-to-open motorcycle assembly line. Less than a month later, on his twenty-ninth birthday, he embarked on his first airplane trip—from Ohio to Kansas City and on to San Francisco. From the Golden Gate City it was destination Tokyo. "They taught another associate and me how to build the CR250 motorcycle," he explains. "I learned how to assemble the front part of the bike while the other associate learned the back half. Before joining Honda, I worked at a motor home manufacturer, and although I owned a motorcycle and tinkered with it, I had no working knowledge whatsoever about how to build one. But I did when I returned to HAM. And it was my responsibility to teach other associates what I had learned."

Yet another associate was only twenty-two years old when he was hired as a welder on HAM's motorcycle assembly line in October 1979. He previously worked for a contractor who built silos for dairy farms. Today, he manages the auto stamping department with 179 people reporting to him. Less than a month after being hired he took a three-week trip to Japan to learn how to weld the frame and rear fork assembly of a new model, the CBX1000. "During my three weeks in Japan, I had to learn all of these processes, collect data, and make up operations manuals to bring back to Marysville so I could train eight associates in the welding department." To date, he has made four trips to Japan. On each trip he studied either motorcycle or automobile procedures, which he later taught to others.

In August 1979, eight months after joining Honda, a twenty-eight-year-old assembly line associate was sent to Japan to study new techniques in building the GL1100 motorcycle. He says he felt enormous pressure because he had to bring home a clear understanding of what he learned, then teach this new knowledge to others. "I felt that since the company believed in me enough to send me to Japan with so much riding on it, I couldn't let them down. I *had* to live up to their expectations!" Hindsight reveals that somebody at Honda showed great vision in entrusting him with his assignment. Today, he is a manager in automobile assembly.

Another twenty-two-year-old man joined Honda after his Navy discharge in July 1980. He, too, started as an associate in the welding department, and today is a coordinator in the auto-stamping department, where six associates report to him. During his second year with the company, he spent sixteen weeks in Japan studying stamping press machinery, the most expensive equipment in the plant. While there, he studied the proper operation of these large machines and, in particular, how to make quick die changes. "Most important, I learned the true meaning of teamwork," he explains. "I also got a firsthand view of Honda's work ethic."

After graduating from the University of Pittsburgh in 1985,

a metallurgy major turned in her cap and gown for a green hat and white uniform. As an engineering staff member, she is responsible for the quality of the steel that comes into the plant. Just three months after she was hired, she was enroute to Tokyo to tour Japanese steel companies. The metallurgist feels her trips (she has been to Japan a second time) have been the most rewarding experiences of her life. "To be given the opportunity to observe some of the world's premier steel companies is a metallurgist's dream come true," she says. "I absorbed so much knowledge—things I never could learn in a classroom or read in a book."

While the above examples represent newly hired associates, large numbers of experienced people are sent each year, particularly when new models are brought out. For instance, when HAM began turning out the new Accord in 1985, the company flew 200 workers representing all areas of the factory to its plant in Sayama, Japan where the new Accord had been in production since spring. The U.S. associates traveled in groups of eight to twenty and stayed for periods ranging from two weeks to three months. They worked side by side with their Japanese associates, and when they returned, they were fully capable of teaching their co-workers.

While these trips were expensive, Honda's investment in its people has paid off in spades. Hundreds of people each year continue to fly to Japan, but as the Marysville work force matures, fewer people will need to make the journey. In fact, when Honda's Alliston, Ontario, plant began production in 1986, every Canadian associate traveled to Ohio for training. This replaced trips to Japan. Interestingly, it is becoming more common today for Japanese employees to visit HAM, not only as teachers, but as students. It's a safe assumption that trips across the Pacific will continue, with American and Japanese associates learning from each other.

A CARING COMPANY

During extensive interviews with hundreds of Honda associates in Ohio, North Carolina, California, and Japan, people proudly acknowledged they knew the company cared about them. While this sense of caring is an intangible and often elusive quality, what a difference it makes. When individuals believe the company sincerely cares about them, they respond by caring about the company. And caring employees are not only more motivated to achieve but also are more conscientious about producing quality work. This multifaceted, caring attitude surfaces again and again as a preeminent theme of Honda and its affiliated companies.

Honda cares. While critics may scowl at this statement and declare it a PR snow job, Honda's caring attitude is as much an integral part of its success story as its technological and marketing achievements. Unfortunately, most people view giant multinational corporations as impersonal and lethargic, yet to date there is no evidence that success or size has adversely affected Honda's devotion to its people. The company's high regard for its associates during the regime of its founders, Soichiro Honda and Takeo Fujisawa, has prevailed and permeated the organization. Honda's present management is working hard to maintain this legacy.

7

*The
Teamwork
Factor*

ANYONE who has participated in a sport recognizes the importance of teamwork; anyone who has watched a football game understands that a winning team must execute every play in harmony. Each of the eleven players must perform with precision or a busted play can result. A missed block, a poorly timed handoff, a bad snap, or an overthrown pass—if only one person fails, the whole team can lose the game.

It's easy to understand the concept of teamwork in sports because we watch it work and we watch it fail every weekend. In every team sport, no matter how outstandingly a single player performs, his or her individual effort probably won't produce winning results unless it is synchronized with the entire team. Similarly, a team of surgeons, a ballet troupe, or an orchestra must work together in perfect harmony—every member doing his or her part, contributing to the whole.

Just as teamwork is a vital and obvious element in winning in athletics, surgery, and the performing arts, so is it an essential ingredient in industry. Yet few managers try to apply it, or they ignore it altogether. Sadly, the lack of teamwork in the workplace causes low productivity and poor quality workmanship—to which many Americans directly attribute the nation's problems in the highly competitive manufacturing arena.

A prevalent school of thought in business circles today is that the Japanese work better together as a team than the Americans do. In part, this is attributed to the Japanese belonging to a homogeneous society. Yet, historically, Americans who came from all corners of the world exerted a strong team effort in building our nation.

Much of Honda's success in the United States is directly related to its ability to inspire teamwork among its American associates. The idea of teamwork and the application of the concept has no national boundaries; it is simply management's job to foster the concept.

NONADVERSARIAL MANAGEMENT

From its beginning, Honda has concentrated on eliminating the pervasive "us" and "them" syndrome that has long been cultivated, and yes, even nurtured by America's automobile manufacturers to segregate white- and blue-collar workers. Such management only divides, never conquers, with "us" remaining hostile to "them." At best, *they* are viewed as uncaring executives who have the time and resources to attend parties and jet about the country. Then, too, because they are of the automotive "nobility," they receive stock options and sizable monetary bonuses—even during the lean years when assembly-line workers are facing massive layoffs.

One outspoken Detroit auto executive recently referred to the "royal class." While it is true that perks have long been the American way, they do not invoke a rapport among the "us" who feel it is highly improbable that such regal status ever will befall them. The "us," therefore, are not motivated to pursue any meaningful or loyal relationship. The inevitable result: rusting panels, loosened bolts, and faulty brakes.

Such a dichotomy of interests makes you wonder how such lavish expenses can subtract from a company's bottom line. And it is hardly surprising that the all-too-familiar phrase

"Have somebody else do it, that's not my job," is heard echoing throughout plants and offices across the United States.

In contrast, Honda creates an environment that cultivates teamwork. The lack of private offices, parking spaces, and dining rooms makes it clear that Honda refuses to divide its people into separate elitist and nonelitist camps. What's more, the 5,700 plus associates at HAM are divided into only two job classifications—production and maintenance. In comparison, some of the unionized American manufacturing plants have as many as a hundred divisions. The benefit is that Honda associates are free to perform many different functions, depending on the production demands in any department.

The lack of barriers separating classes is a direct result of founder Soichiro Honda's bedrock philosophy of treating people as equals. "I associate with anybody—rich or poor," he said. "It doesn't make any difference. I prefer to have the principle of egalitarianism rather than a class distinction of people. The most important thing in the world is not diamonds or gold, but humans. And everybody has to learn about humans. To do that, we must have a broad contact."

Soichiro Honda practiced what he preached. He believed that managers should demonstrate good leadership by performing the most undesirable jobs at least once. Accordingly, he was known to sweep the factory floors, empty ashtrays, and pick up paper towels on the restroom floors.

From the onset, newly hired associates are made to feel part of the team. A preorientation period is held for new associates, during which family members can attend in order to understand the high level of commitment that the job requires. Later, HAM shows several orientation films about the company. As one new associate put it, "Even these company movies constantly referred to everyone as 'we.' I felt I was joining something very special."

The stress on *we* is hammered home during the indoctrination, and once on the factory floor, associates discover it's not just lip service. The distinction between manager and worker is subtle. Some recently hired people complained that their first weeks on the job were informal compared with their previous jobs. One HAM associate explained: "It takes a while to get used to being treated decently at work." There sometimes appears to be confusion and a lack of order in the beginning, but there is a trade-off: Everyone feels he or she belongs on the same team.

THE TEAM LEADER

Unlike a shop foreman, the team leader doesn't "boss" anyone. Like a utility baseball player whose enthusiastic infield chatter inspires the entire squad, the team leader infuses the team with spirit and can fill in during absences. An associate can be promoted to this position after working at HAM for at least twelve months, and he or she guides and serves rather than orders and demands. Still, the position is a promotion and includes an hourly pay raise of 65 cents. The size of a team can range from five to twenty associates, but twelve is about average. A team works together in a specific area or department. Team leaders report to coordinators, who each supervise four or five teams. Each team has a specific function. For example, one team installs drive train components. Another team might assemble instrument panels, while other teams work in the paint, welding, stamping, and quality control departments.

The responsibilities of a team leader are many and their talents are varied. He or she is capable of performing every job in his or her unit, and accordingly, trains new associates. Because absenteeism at HAM runs about 2 percent—and there are no worker reserves—the team leader may serve as a "spare player" and substitute for a missing associate. Because there are no workers "waiting in the wings," it becomes necessary for every associate to come to work every day. Most important, the team leader is right on the spot, and should a problem arise, he or she has a good understanding of it and can usually find a solution.

The day typically begins for a team leader about thirty minutes before the first shift begins production at 6:30 A.M. In addition to reviewing the previous shift's reports, the team leader will check the team's area to be certain all tools and parts are available. Then he or she inspects equipment. As one team leader in HAM's auto assembly department says: "I don't want my members to worry about the availability of parts or production equipment. We must prepare for a smooth start-up and flow of operations." She conducts a five- to ten-minute meeting with the sixteen members of her team each morning, discussing safety items or problems that might have occurred the previous day, exchanging ideas, and reviewing the day's production goals and how best to reach them. When her shift ends at 3:00 P.M., she completes her daily reports for the second shift team leader before leaving.

A common expression at HAM is, "Accept no bad parts, make no bad parts, pass no bad parts." The team leader understands this phrase well, and accordingly, it's his or her responsibility to communicate with other departments when a team member uncovers any less-than-perfect parts.

Finally, the saying, "The speed of the pack is the speed of the leader" is appropriate when describing a good team leader. Not only does the team leader set the pace by exemplifying good work habits and excellence but if someone falls behind on the line he or she will step in to lend a helping hand. Other associates will then do the same.

Several training programs are available to all associates and team leaders. These programs play a key role in the advancement of associates—more than 90 percent of those promoted began their careers on the shop floor. Being a team leader is an excellent position for developing good leadership qualities, and serves as an outstanding breeding ground for future Honda managers.

ROTATING JOBS

It's not unusual for the traditional factory worker to begin his or her career doing a specific job, and thirty years later still be doing primarily the same work.

HAM rotates associates from job to job within each team, thus avoiding situations in which tedious work causes boredom, which, in turn, might lead to deteriorating morale and quality. A new job often rejuvenates enthusiasm. Job rotation also increases one's overall knowledge of production, so if a particular process becomes obsolete, an associate who is flexible will not. For instance, if a fork-lift operator is trained only to operate a fork lift, and a conveyor system is installed, the associate would lose his or her job. However, if the same associate is trained to handle parts and materials in various ways, he or she can more easily switch positions. Thus, job rotation promotes job security.

There are two other important advantages to Honda's job rotations. First, the more jobs an associate can handle, the better his or her understanding of the manufacturing process, which makes the associate more valuable to the company. When workers are rotated from job to job within a team, they become fully capable of performing all of the functions performed by other team members and can better relate their work to everyone else's. This understanding also promotes good teamwork—once people understand how their tasks fit into the whole picture, they can come up with ways to improve operations for the entire team.

Managers, too, are frequently transferred to different departments—sometimes very different from their previous assignments. For instance, Steve Powell, who is the present manager of the automobile paint department, began his career at HAM as an associate assemblying dirt bikes in 1979. The following year, he was transferred to the engine repair area, and after a trip to Japan for some training, he became a production coordinator. Shortly after the automobile plant opened in 1984, Powell was named production coordinator responsible for a section of its assembly line, although he says, "I knew absolutely nothing about putting a car together." He later became an assistant manager in the automobile assembly department, and then, in 1986, he was appointed manager of the automobile paint department. Again he claims, "I knew absolutely nothing about painting a car." There's a good reason why Honda transfers its people to different departments. When managers have a good understanding about many facets of the manufacturing process, they are better able to work with other departments. And cooperation among departments is essential in a manufacturing plant.

THE RACING SPIRIT

In recent years, Honda has excelled in more motorcycle and automobile racing events than perhaps any other company in the world. With such a strong commitment to racing comes the prestige and immediate recognition of Honda products. Then too, advanced technology is required to excel in world-class racing events, and Honda has used that technology in its new-product designs. Most important, the Honda racing spirit serves as the basis of its managerial philosophy.

A strong winner-take-all attitude is necessary to compete successfully in a world-class racing event. In a race, a specific goal is established—to be number one. With this in mind, all members of the team know they must work together to reach this goal. And, in a race, the team has a definite, limited framework in which to work, so goals must be reached quickly. The racing environment is an excellent training ground for developing superior engineers and superior managers.

To win a Formula One race in the highly competitive worldwide arena, the teamwork among the driver, mechanics, and engineers is essential. If the mechanic fails to do his or her job, the driver has no chance. If the engineers fail to design the car properly, the mechanic has no chance. All are dependent on each other. There's no guarantee that a race will be won with the fastest car, the best mechanics, and the most highly skilled driver. The team also must communicate. If the driver cannot explain correctly what is wrong, if the mechanics and engineers cannot understand the real problem, then they probably will lose the race.

Racing also is a highly unpredictable sport. When a problem arises, a quick solution is mandatory. And if it's a problem that hasn't occurred before, the team must have enough flexibility and ingenuity to come up with a new solution on the spot.

Answers must be found in split seconds. When people learn to work together in a challenging environment, they perform at peak levels.

Likewise, good communication and quick resolve are necessary ingredients in the highly competitive manufacturing arena. When equipment in the plant is not operating properly, the line will stop. Maintenance people must move instantly to fix the problem and associates must be prepared to make up for lost time. So, for good reason, downtime in a Honda manufacturing plant is measured in seconds, not minutes or hours. At HAM, a problem becomes a critical pit stop.

The lessons Honda learns on the race track are applied in the plant because, as Irimajiri says, "The effort involved in building an automobile is the same brand of teamwork, but on a larger scale. The effort to design, engineer, manufacture, and sell a car involves thousands of people from different cultures and languages. And when we bring out a new model with features superior to those of our competitors', and do so ahead of them, there is no doubt that we're in a race and that we intend to win."

A NONUNION SHOP

Unlike most domestic auto makers, a union does not exist at HAM. And while it's a safe assumption that Honda prefers to operate a nonunion shop, management takes no official position on the subject. Officially, and quite reasonably, it's a matter the company says is entirely up to its associates.

A brief glance at the history of unions in this country reveals that in their early days industry abused labor. Unions formed to protect and represent the working men and women. With unions came many positive changes, including the abolishment of child labor, improved working conditions, higher levels of safety, and labor's right to voice an opinion without fear of retribution. Henceforth, management could no longer treat workers as machinery. Collectively, workers could effectively bargain to improve their lives.

But one school of thought believes the pendulum now has swung the other way. Some believe that unions have made unreasonable demands on management, destroying many companies' competitive edges. This has led many to question whether some unions actually serve and benefit the work force. It is not the intention of this book to settle such a debate, but rather to suggest that each company should be individually scrutinized regarding the pros and cons of unionization. Some work forces may benefit; others may not.

We can, however, safely assume that workers will have less need for unions if their employers treat them well. Note, for example, that IBM is America's largest nonunion employer; its people are paid well, are content, and are highly motivated. Likewise, the better treatment associates receive at HAM, the less need they may have for a union. As one associate put it, "There's a price—union dues. Why should I pay to have a union represent me when I'm quite satisfied with how the company treats me now?" Obviously, employees have less incentive to pay for representation when their working conditions are favorable.

In fact, HAM associates already receive pay equal to that of union workers. This is especially true when you consider that all HAM associates received an additional $11.84 each for every $100 they earned during 1986 for sharing Honda's worldwide profits. Add overtime, which ranges from time-and-a-half to triple pay, plus monthly attendance bonuses, and there are few financial incentives to being unionized.

As long as Honda managers and associates continue to work in harmony, it is unlikely that a union will ever come close to getting its foot in the door at HAM. Since its first plant opened in 1979, the United Auto Workers (UAW) has been trying to organize HAM's work force, but has made virtually no progress.

It did have one minor victory, however, in 1982 when the National Labor Relations Board ruled against Honda's policy of banning union caps on the job. Even so, only a handful of union hats are visible today in the sea of green and white caps.

And, on occasion, when a union hat or two is spotted, it generally is worn as a means of voicing a complaint, not to seriously invite unionization.

A union probably won't get a strong foothold at HAM anytime soon, but what if it did? How would a union affect job rotation and the team spirit, where everyone pitches in to help fellow associates build the highest-quality products possible?

If associates unionize at HAM, it would have to be a different type of union than presently exists in many American factories. If not, the wonderful team spirit could vanish.

A SPIRIT OF PRIDE

From the evidence of more than a hundred interviews with Honda employees and observing associates in plants and offices throughout the United States and Japan, it's apparent that the people who work for this company feel as though they, themselves, are winners. It's a rare spirit in our American business world. Like the warm connection people feel toward their high schools and colleges, the enduring spirit generates a proud feeling, a feeling of belonging to something special.

As one associate describes the spirit, "It comes from knowing that if we all pull together, we will put out a superior product. It's *us* who make it happen." And another associate expressed how proud she feels when she watches each car roll off the assembly line, "knowing that I was part of it." The same applies when a HAM associate sees a Honda car and looks to see if it was built here or in Japan. There's a definite competitive spirit that prevails within Honda, a friendly rivalry between the Japanese and Americans about who produces better products. As if the other automobile companies aren't stiff enough competition, Honda factories must compete with each other.

A winning spirit inspires people to pull together for the sake of the team. In 1985, a team of six welders wanted to play radios on the job, but they voted against asking for the privilege because, as one said, "After you work on the plant's stamping press machines for a while, you can tell just by the sound whether the job has been done right." With the radios playing, the group thought it would not be possible to detect such sounds.

How does a company instill such a sense of pride in its people? To some degree, it starts at the top and filters down. Perhaps it's reflected in the deep pride that company president Shoichiro Irimajiri has in HAM's products. It is he who proudly drives a new model of the Gold Wing off the assembly line and then numerous laps around a high-speed test track as part of a special ceremony honoring the occasion. It's a safe bet that few new motorcycles or cars have ever been so ceremoniously tested.

Irimajiri demonstrated how he feels about the associates when he was invited to the annual Automotive Hall of Fame dinner in Detroit in October 1986 and again in 1987. About 600 of the industry's highest-ranking executives attended the plush banquet that year. Rather than taking top HAM managers, Irimajiri went with six production associates. They chartered a private plane for the affair, and they spent the evening hobnobbing with the automobile industry's elite. You can bet no other production workers were present that night. You also can bet that no one at that banquet was prouder than those six associates and Shoichiro Irimajiri.

8

Instilling Pride

PEOPLE don't seem to care about the quality of their work anymore" is an all-too-frequent complaint that echoes throughout the country today. And who, while shopping in a department store, or waiting for the mechanic to finish a tune-up, or standing in line at an airline counter, hasn't muttered to themselves: "Whatever happened to good service?"

No one can deny that pride has disappeared from many American workplaces today, but what can be done to rejuvenate it? In particular, what can a company do to instill pride in its people so they care enough to perform their best?

From the consumer's point of view, pride in workmanship begins with superior products and better service, desirable objectives for any enterprise. From a company's viewpoint, employees who feel good about themselves, who have inner pride and self-esteem, become more productive people. And increased productivity shows up where it counts—on the company's bottom line.

A QUALITY PRODUCT—A SOURCE OF PRIDE

A definite correlation exists between the quality of a company's products and the pride of a company's employees. In short, people feel good about themselves when they know their product represents a good value to the customer. Similarly, people have low self-esteem when they work for a company known for inferior merchandise. The degree of pride people take in their work is directly affected by how they are perceived, or think they are perceived, by the community.

In interview after interview at HAM, people expressed a true sense of pride in themselves because they were part of a team that produced a fine product. And feeling good about their product generated good feelings about themselves. As one associate on the automobile assembly line expressed, "Since I started working here, I notice with pride every Honda that goes by on the road." Other associates commented on the favorable recognition they receive when they tell others they work for Honda. A stamping coordinator said, "The demand for a job here is far greater than the number of openings, so it's quite prestigious to be employed here." And even in Columbus, an hour's drive from HAM, associates claimed, "Whenever I'm in a gathering of people, at a party, for instance, all I have to do is mention to someone where I work, and I automatically become the topic of conversation. Everyone wants to know what it's like to work for Honda."

Certainly, it's a good feeling for anyone to be identified in a positive way with a company that enjoys a reputation for quality products. Sadly, however, it's the exception rather than the rule for people to regard their employer so highly. Too often, employees avoid discussing their work: Insurance agents fear somebody will complain about a mishandled claim; manufacturers' employees want to avoid the subject of warranties that weren't honored; retail salespeople shy away from conversations about false advertising claims; and so on. An Ohio Honda dealer says, "It's a wonderful feeling to be able to sell a product to somebody and not have to make excuses. I feel comfortable selling a Honda to my friends. In the past, I felt embarrassed to be associated with some of the domestic cars I sold." Honda people welcome the chance to talk about their company. So do members of their families. An associate who works in the plastics department says: "For show-and-tell, both of my daughters wore Honda hats and my work shirts to school. They're proud that their mom works for Honda."

The automobile industry's highly respected J. D. Powers survey ranked Honda cars number one, overtaking Mercedes-Benz in customer satisfaction in 1986. The following year, Honda's entry "slipped" to the number two spot in the Powers ratings, relinquishing the top spot to Honda's Acura line. An assistant purchasing manager comments on the rankings, "Those ratings make me puff up and say I'm really proud to be here."

NEVER COMPROMISE ON QUALITY

When Steve Yoder, the motorcycle group manager in charge of new models, first joined Honda in August 1979, he was one of only fourteen associates working on the new plant's assembly line. Following a few weeks of training, production of the first Honda motorcycle, the CR250, was underway. At the time, one of his responsibilities was installing the fuel tank and, in particular, making certain its rubber O ring was properly sealed. Following his inspection, Yoder was told to use a magic marker to put a check mark on the fuel cock, which was then inserted into the fuel tank.

"I didn't understand the need to put the check mark on the fuel cock before it went into the fuel tank," Yoder tells, "so I asked one of the other engineers what he thought about it. 'It's up to you,' he said, so I stopped doing it.

"A couple of days later, an engineer from Japan who supervised the assembly department asked me why I wasn't putting the marks on the fuel cocks. I explained that I didn't see any reason to do it. He then told me that an inspector further down the line was required to look at the bottom of the tank for the mark to be certain that it had been inspected. 'The double check is done,' he said, 'because if there was a gasoline leak, a fire might occur.' My mark informed the inspector that I had inspected it twice.

"The engineer wanted to make sure I wouldn't make the same mistake again. So somebody else was put in my place on the assembly line, and I was to inspect every motorcycle that had been built after the point when I stopped doing the check marks. This meant I had to take the fuel cock out of seventy-five motorcycles, look at the O ring, then put each back in again. And yes, I made sure to put my mark on every single one of them the second time around."

Although he didn't find a single gasoline tank with a potential leak, Yoder did learn an important lesson, one that was taught to him in a firm but gentle manner. Nobody came down hard on him for his mistake, but he received a full explanation about *why* the inspection was necessary.

As soon as HAM was satisfied with the quality of its CR250 dirt bike production, the manufacture of its deluxe touring motorcycle, known as the Gold Wing, began. The Gold Wing was top of the line, and the associates, many of whom were motorcycle buffs, clearly understood the necessity for this product to be perfect. Throughout production of Honda's most prestigious bike, the focus was on quality and the priority at HAM has been the same since then. This first group of Americans in motorcycle production formed a nucleus of dedicated associates, many of whom later were transferred to the automobile plant. From this small unit, other highly conscientious associates were developed.

The emphasis on the Gold Wing's quality is well illustrated by its first assembly at HAM. A small scratch was found on its chrome mufflers. When the scratch was discovered, many associates didn't think anything of it—it could be seen only if somebody was on his or her hands and knees looking underneath the motorcycle.

"But if one customer does get down on his hands and knees and sees it, we have a problem," a vice-president said. With that, a half day's production was lost while the scratched mufflers were replaced. As it turned out, the mufflers were scratched while being removed from crates due to poor packaging.

As HAM vice-president Al Kinzer emphasizes, "From the very beginning, before we ever built the first motorcycle here, we kept repeating that our top priority is to make a quality product. We've made this message perfectly clear to everyone. It was, and is, a precise goal of what we want to accomplish.

"Now, I think people want to believe in management," Kinzer continues. "They want to believe management is sincere and means what it says. But for this to happen, it's paramount that management practices what it says. To paraphrase Ralph Waldo Emerson: 'What you are thunders, for I cannot hear what you say.' I believe the meaning of this quote is what separates Honda and our people from many other organizations and their people. When it comes to quality, we never compromise. *Never.* There is only one standard that is acceptable and it never varies.

"It's so easy to let people off the hook in the heat of the day when you're being pushed. So you always must remember that no product, under any circumstances, ever goes out the door if quality is compromised. You can't say, 'Okay, shipping must go on today. Just this one time we'll slacken our standards and let the car go out the door, and we'll hope and we'll pray that it will go unnoticed.' Once you do, you've taught your people that a double standard exists, one that's dependent upon how management feels at a particular time. Once you do that, you've violated your rules on what your real objective is, and you've lost it. And once it's lost, you can never get it back. Your people are confused, and they no longer understand what you truly want to accomplish."

Kinzer believes most people don't have to be coerced into working. "They're willing to work, and in general, they have pride in what they do when standards have been set for them to meet. Then, by participating in what is on par with those standards, they feel proud of their accomplishments. Anything less simply isn't good enough."

This attention to quality is carried to what some may consider extremes. For example, the finish of a car might have a small blemish that could be seen only when the light is shining on it a certain way. No matter: It will be pulled off the line to be repaired.

There's no doubt that quality is the top priority at HAM, clearly having precedence even over productivity. Bob Simcox, assistant plant manager, recognizes this well. For instance, a problem once occurred on the welding line with a little metal strip behind the rear door where the side panel joins the roof panel. Its position was off by about a millimeter and Simcox worried about the appearance. Not satisfied that he was getting the proper results from countermeasures, he ordered the entire weld shop shut down until a correction could be made. It's rare—and expensive—to shut down an entire department. Add the lost production to the payroll expense required to pay a couple of hundred people for the lost time and it was easy to see that Simcox had made a difficult decision.

"But I didn't have any alternative," he says. "I wasn't satisfied with the quality, so the problem had to be solved."

Just as associates understand the high standards the company expects them to reach, so do its vendors. Although buying parts at competitive prices is essential, quality is Honda's top priority. It's the responsibility of the purchasing department to seek out suppliers with the right people, processes, and technology to produce a quality part. In its effort to buy parts made in the United States, Honda's people regularly visit potential suppliers throughout the country. A remark often heard from potential suppliers is "This is what we make for your competitor in Detroit, and our product is good enough for them so it should be good enough for you." This doesn't work with Honda. As one purchasing manager put it, "We have to be better because we're competing against them." Some suppliers take the attitude, "Our job is to give you the parts, and *you* must check the quality." Honda replies, "That is not enough; we expect 100 percent good parts." To improve quality, Honda began sending its engineers to help its suppliers boost quality.

With Honda working closely with a vendor, the vendor's quality and technology can be vastly improved. Because of the company's reputation for insisting on quality, it has become a source of pride within the industry to be known as a Honda supplier.

Bellemar Parts Industries, an automobile seat manufacturer just down the road from HAM, offers a good example of what happens when a supplier runs into a delivery problem. Bellemar's supplier of foam was running late on a delivery due to a truck breakdown and the supply of foam was nearly exhausted. With the prospect of the Honda assembly line shutting down only a few hours away, it was clear that immediate action needed to be taken. To keep the line running, the foam supplier shipped the materials by a private airline carrier. When the supplies arrived in Columbus, they immediately were loaded on a helicopter and airlifted to Bellemar. Once the seats were made at Bellemar, they were loaded on a truck and brought to HAM, where associates individually carried them down the line to be installed in each car. It was costly for the material to be delivered by the supplier at its expense, but it had to be done. While Bellemar was scrambling, cars were rolling down the assembly line sans seats. Fortunately, the seats were installed later and the need to shut down the line was averted.

BEING YOUR OWN QUALITY INSPECTOR

From day one, associates are told, "The quality and acceptance of Honda products is our job security." The message is made clear that employment depends on superior products. And to accomplish this objective, each individual must do his or her best to assure quality.

Associates are an irreplaceable part of the process of building quality products. At every level, people feel as though they make valuable contributions to the company, and they know that quality rests on their shoulders. No quality inspectors are breathing down anyone's back or looking over shoulders. What's more, not only do associates inspect their own work but they are encouraged to look for defects that occurred elsewhere in the manufacturing process. Associates feel as though they have a vested interest in what's produced in the entire factory. There are few ill feelings when somebody discovers something wrong in somebody else's work. It's a team effort and all members of the team benefit.

As Scott Whitlock, HAM senior vice-president and auto

plant manager, explains, "Our people have a real understanding that our success and future is dependent upon the quality of the products we make today. Although HAM is a manufacturing plant, I like to think of us as a marketing arm. I tell this to our people and point out that every car we send out today ultimately results in somebody being either satisfied or dissatisfied. And when we have satisfied customers, they are going to come back to buy their next cars from us, and they also will tell their friends to buy cars from us. Our marketing data shows that repeat business and referrals are two principle sources for a high percentage of our sales. I think it's important for our manufacturing people to realize how the quality of their work relates directly to the customer."

Evidently, HAM associates do recognize this. The following comments reflect the pride expressed by some of the associates:

> The paint job is the first thing that people notice about a car. And when I see a Honda driving down the street and the paint looks great, I get this feeling inside that everybody can see what we have done.
>
> —Paint department associate

> When I see a Honda going down the road, I know that I played a part in making it. With some companies, like a tire manufacturer, a person actually signs his name to the tire. We don't sign our names to the cars, but we have the same feeling of pride.
>
> —Assembly line coordinator

> In 1984, HAM's motto was: "We ourselves make success and security certain by satisfying our customers." Our people live by that. Everyone is a quality inspector and that's why so few defects ever get through the line.
>
> —Welding department team leader

> Everyone naturally wants to do a good job and has a lot of pride when he does things right. But you have to let the

guy do it. I think the traditional domestic auto worker has been knocked down so many times by bureaucracy and red tape that he simply gives up. The worker thinks it's up to somebody else, and he can't change anything even when he wants to.

—Quality control engineer

QUALITY CONTROL

While it is true that inspectors don't stand tyrannically behind associates prejudging and rejudging their work, this does not imply that quality control is missing at HAM. Even before the assembly line starts rolling, the quality control department is constantly inspecting new parts as they arrive at the plant. If a problem is revealed, the vendor immediately is informed whether it is a Japanese or domestic supplier. Checkpoints down the line detect work that does not meet Honda's standards. However, as the manager of HAM's auto quality control department points out, "While it's our job to confirm the degree of quality that exists, the quality has to be built into each car. It's not possible for us to uncover every mistake. Quality control can serve only as a net. We'll catch only so much and the rest will go through."

As cars are moving down the assembly line, associates are inspecting their own work and checking for defects that may have occurred further up the line. The quality control department inspects each car at the end of the assembly line and minor problems are fixed by designated mechanics. Every car goes through a series of inspections for about fifteen minutes with about thirty people checking it out. These inspectors do everything from looking under the hood and inside the car to rolling the windows up and down, from closing doors to examining latches, from testing brakes to making sure all the switches work. The car is run on a dynamometer, sprayed with water to test for leaks, and *road tested. Every* car is driven over a two-mile test track during its final inspection. Most automobile manufacturers conduct only random test drives.

Approximately 60 percent of all cars rolling off the assembly line don't pass through quality control without some sort of problem being spotted. To the uninitiated, this number may seem to reflect a poor product. In reality, it is a reflection of Honda's intolerance of defects of any kind. In most cases the repair department must make only minor adjustments.

The quality control manager explains, "In the long run it's really the responsibility of the associates on the line to do their jobs according to the company's high standards." When a problem is discovered, quality control must communicate that error back to its source. The quickest feedback is needed because long delays in relaying the message will end with cars piling up bumper-to-bumper with the same defect. For this reason, Honda believes it is absolutely necessary to have a totally integrated manufacturing operation—one in which stamping, welding, painting, plastic injection molding, and assembly are combined under one roof. For example, if a problem occurs in welding that involves stamped parts, the welding staff simply walks over to the stamping department to quickly solve the problem. In other companies, it is not unusual for the stamping plant to be many miles away from assembly operations.

SOME THOUGHTFUL PERKS

HAM has a package of employee benefits including profit sharing and various insurance coverages. While these are valuable "perks," many other companies also provide them. It is, perhaps, Honda's other "extras" that demonstrate how the company cares about its people. These added touches are not necessary for a company to be competitive in the job market but nevertheless do serve as daily reminders that HAM is a nice place to work. The following are examples.

There is a recreation center consisting of a showplace health club with a 25-meter, six-lane swimming pool, a fifteen-person whirlpool, a 12,000-square-foot basketball court that converts into two volleyball courts, a state-of-the-art workout area with the finest weight-lifting equipment, and a 2,000-square-foot party room equipped with a full kitchen that associates can reserve for private functions. Both the men's and women's locker rooms have saunas. A staff of seven operates the center, which had 63,000 visits by associates during 1986. For those who like outdoor activities, plans call for building a one-mile jogging track around the sports complex. Also on site is an outdoor recreation area, with picnic parks, baseball diamonds, and an eleven-acre pond, to be well stocked and have piers for associates who enjoy fishing. Two pavilions, complete with picnic tables and grills, accommodate an outing big enough for a hundred or more people. And for the children, there are swings and slides.

A service center occupies a deluxe 19,000-square-foot garage where master mechanics service employees' automobiles. The service center offers competitively priced gasoline, a coin-operated automatic car wash, and do-it-yourself repair bays for employees who like to tinker with their cars and motorcycles. In addition to special discounts they receive on all Honda products, employee-purchased automobiles are delivered and serviced through the center. Parts and accessories for Honda automobiles are available, as is warranty service work. A credit union is in the service center and has a convenient drive-up window for transactions.

HONDA: THE CORPORATE CITIZEN

Being a participating citizen in the community where the company conducts its business is part of Honda's international philosophy. It's a matter of honor, a dictate that each individual must pay his or her dues. If a person takes something out of the community, he or she must put something back. So must a corporation.

While Honda has made numerous donations over the years, the following is a description of a cross-section of some of the more unusual and thoughtful contributions.

Hurricane Camille, which hit Gulfport and Biloxi, Mississippi, in 1969 with 200 mph winds, killed at least 300 people, left 200,000 homeless, and destroyed $1 billion worth of property. Americans throughout the nation helplessly watched the catastrophe on television, anxiously viewing the strongest storm ever to strike the United States. Two thousand miles away in Gardena, California, American Honda officials weren't content to sit and watch, so they contacted the National Red Cross in Washington and volunteered to lend generators for power, water pumps, and all-terrain vehicles that could travel on otherwise inaccessible roads. After the Red Cross accepted the contribution, southeastern Honda distributors helped deliver the supplies. A Honda dealer in Mobile arranged for the National Guard to fly everything to Biloxi, and the dealer's sales and service people uncrated and checked the equipment to make sure it worked.

To help reduce the teenage drug problem in the United States, the company in 1964 lent a helping hand to a youth center for troubled boys in a blighted eastern Los Angeles neighborhood. Honda donated several mini-bikes to the center and required each boy to sign a contract that allowed him to ride one of the bikes. In the contract, each boy promised to attend school regularly, stay off drugs, and obey the laws. With good behavior, he could *earn* the right to operate a mini-bike. The response was tremendous, and delinquency dropped significantly throughout the community. The program subsequently led to the formation of the National Youth Using Mini-Bike Program. Working through YMCAs, Honda dealers across the United States have donated more than 12,000 mini-bikes.

In "Educators to Japan," five Ohio school districts each select a Teacher of the Year to visit Japan, courtesy of Honda. One or two HAM associates usually accompany each teacher as traveling companions and company goodwill ambassadors. These trips help develop a better understanding between the two countries' people.

For several years, Honda has worked with a rehabilitation center for young paraplegics and quadriplegics in California. In addition to donating money and company products, which are used for fund-raising, Honda employees devote a lot of their time.

Votech is a national program through which Honda sends service division instructors to vocational schools. Honda donates motorcycle engines and generators so teachers can learn how to repair Honda engines. They, in turn, can teach others.

Honda has adopted the Gardena Elementary School in a California Adopt-a-School program, and coordinates a mini–Rose Bowl Parade for the school. Willie Tokishi, who heads American Honda's community relations department, says, "We teach the kids how to apply teamwork, a valuable lesson for young people." Some of the judges who officiate the real Rose Bowl Parade in Pasadena are brought in to judge the float entries and award prizes ranging from tee-shirts to hats. Honda also helps the elementary school put together a yearbook.

For years, Honda has entered a float in the Rose Bowl Parade. One vice-president said: "The float is our season's greeting card to America and our way to say, 'Thank-you.'"

Each year, American Honda has a community fair day in the parking lot of its California headquarters and all local civic and charitable organizations that the company supports have booths. The fair teaches employees about the company's participation in community affairs, and encourages them to become involved.

9

People Involvement

YEARS AGO, Soichiro Honda addressed the question: "How can we motivate our production people to feel the same way about their jobs as our managers do?"

His concern was by no means revolutionary. Management has long sought new and improved ways to inspire workers to perform at higher levels. Just how this objective is reached, however, differs vastly from manager to manager. Styles of leadership range from lax to dictatorial. While neither extreme is satisfactory, the latter is the more common; overbearing and intimidating managerial techniques are the rule, not the exception.

Rather than callously controlling its work force, Honda permits its people to have more say about their jobs. The manager of associate development at HAM explains: "We want associates to use their heads as well as their hands. When a company uses only its people's hands, it's merely buying them. But when the company solicits their thoughts, their hearts eventually are won because then people have a total commitment to their company."

The department head doesn't believe it's possible for managers to control employees. He says, "It's the associates who have the control, and for them to do their best work they must fully understand their jobs and give their full commitment. It's not realistic to expect management to continually keep tabs on a few thousand associates on the production line."

Some experts credit much of Honda's success to its ability to get people involved. The more involved people are, the more they give to their employer.

THE THINKING ASSOCIATE

"Nobody knows your job better than you do," Honda associates repeatedly are told. What's more, because they are considered experts at their jobs, associates are encouraged to improve their work.

What separates Honda's associates from other factory workers is that they are authorized to think. They aren't on the line performing by rote, going through the motions, working like zombies. Soichiro Honda said many years ago, "A man's ability can never be replaced by a machine." He believed that machines were tools for relieving tedium in automotive plants. The same applies today. The company wants innovative associates, people who can solve problems, devise ways to work more efficiently, and improve the quality of its products. It seeks thinking people who can react quickly in emergency situations.

A thinking work force! Imagine having feedback from thousands of people who are right there on the job, each thinking about ways to do things a little better, to save a little time and a little money for the company. The collective mind of a company's work force can be its most valuable asset. Smart management takes advantage of this.

How does a company maximize this precious resource, which, to a large degree, is not properly used in American industry? One way is to let people know their thoughts sincerely are wanted. A firm must demonstrate a willingness to listen to ideas. Again, it boils down to having respect for the individual. Sometimes, to analyze a particular production process, HAM will videotape the job process at the work station. Later, the associates in that job process area will review the videotape and ask questions such as: "What do you think?" "Do you think you can save some time by doing this some other way?" "What ideas do you get from this tape that would help you do your job better?" Other times, team leaders, coordinators, and some division managers attend classes in supervisory skills to discuss a single subject. For instance, one class may spend two hours airing views on "What is a good coordinator?" During one of these sessions, several different perspectives are presented.

Honda understands that people are more likely to come up with fresh ideas when they're in a creative atmosphere. This is particularly true when they know management cares about their thoughts, and they know they could make a difference. Not only must their ideas be heard but when good ones are presented they must be implemented. Passive, unresponsive listening eventually destroys people's incentive for expressing their thoughts.

Honda contradicts the common western belief that the Japanese think collectively and discourage individualism. Honda places a strong emphasis on the value of each associate. Soichiro Honda said, "Nonconformity is essential to an artist or inventor."

A thinking work force must be given the freedom to take risks. When people are afraid to make mistakes, they will continually repeat the same processes. The fear of trying to do things differently short-circuits creativity.

One HAM manager learned during his early days when he was working in the motorcycle plant that anything less than excellence was unacceptable. "The paint department was having trouble keeping up with the production line because the decals kept bubbling on the motorcycles, causing us to work overtime," the manager recalls. "I discussed the problem with an executive vice-president of the plant, telling him, 'I am sorry, but we're doing what we can to solve the problem.' The executive vice-president looked at me and said in a soft voice, 'It's easy to say you're sorry, but it is difficult to solve a problem.' I got the message and will always remember it. At the time, I would have preferred that he yell at me, but it was his quiet and firm way to tell me that I was responsible for solving the problem that made the difference. Sure, it put pressure on me because *I* had to get some quick results. I didn't have the luxury to take all day to figure out a solution. Yet, at the same time, I had a good feeling inside because it was up to me to solve the problem."

To those outsiders who stereotype Japanese management, it is difficult to comprehend that Honda nurtures a free-spirit atmosphere. Similarly confusing is the incongruity that exists between the company's teamwork philosophy and the nonconformity concept. Yet teamwork and individuality do work hand-in-hand at Honda. While individual stardom is not sought, performing at one's peak level is highly lauded.

NO JOB DESCRIPTIONS

There are very vague job descriptions for the newly hired associates at HAM. While a lack of strong supervision may cause confusion and frustration in the beginning of one's career with the company, the vast majority of associates eventually adjust to the system.

One engineer, who now develops specifications for plant equipment, talks about his first few months at HAM. "Following my graduation from the university, I was hired in with a group of ten other engineers, and we worked on the assembly line for a three-month period in three different departments. My first assignment was in Motorcycle Quality Control, then I was transferred to Automobile Quality Control, which was followed by a stint in Motorcycle Assembly. Each time, I worked on the line learning the nuts and bolts of the business. Now, I don't think a graduate engineer would be put on the line at General Motors. Throughout my training, the company was vague about defining my responsibilities and what was expected of me. Each member in our group kept asking over and over, 'What do you expect us to do?' But we never were given specific answers. Our managers expected us to know what we were to do and assume the responsibility. Of course, now I know they left it broad on purpose. That's the way Honda does it. But in the meantime, it was very frustrating, and one of the guys in the group couldn't hack it and resigned. He needed a job description and was lost without one. It's been two years, and I and the others are doing quite well."

An engineering division manager said, "My first boss gave me the best advice I've ever received. During my first week, I commented on how difficult it was for me to understand what my actual job was. He looked at me silently for a few seconds and then said in a low voice, 'Your job is everything.' That was it! Not another word and he walked away. It took me a while to realize what he meant and how right on target he was."

As several HAM associates said, while it initially is difficult to adapt, the lack of job descriptions offers a freedom to grow. An attitude prevails that job descriptions actually restrain people. Without them, the possibilities are infinite. While people do have an understanding about their day-to-day activities, it's quite clear "there are no limits. You should do, and you should grow and develop in many directions."

The vague job descriptions are perhaps even more pronounced at higher levels of management. Toshi Amino, executive vice-president at HAM, who started his Honda career in Tokyo in the domestic sales department, explains, "In 1980, I was assigned to a project team to help get the automobile plant constructed in Marysville. Initially, I was sent to Ohio for three weeks. It was to be a very temporary position.

"When I first arrived here, I asked the project leader what my job was. He replied, 'Well, you worked in America before, so you know this country. Maybe you can find something that you can do.'

"That's the way it is here. You get involved in a particular area where you have an interest. Soon I started working with the negotiations with the engineers and the contractors, and spent the majority of my time with the construction of the automobile plant. By the end of 1982, when the construction was about completed, I was named vice-president of Bellemar Parts Industries, a subsidiary company down the road from HAM, jointly owned by Honda and two Japanese suppliers. In May 1987, I became HAM's executive vice-president and my work includes administration, accounting, data processing, corporate planning, corporate communications, purchasing, etc. So while I started out in the marketing end of the business, I am now in the manufacturing area. And what was a three-week temporary assignment has become a permanent assignment."

When job descriptions spell everything out to the letter, workers are likely to do only what they're *supposed* to do, and nothing more. So when something goes wrong in a factory, workers typically go to their supervisors and explain what happened. In turn, a foreman has somebody fix it, or if it's not too complicated, gives instructions on how to do it. At HAM, management approaches problems very differently. When a problem is presented to a manager, a series of questions probably will follow: "Exactly what went wrong?" "Why did it happen?" "What are the consequences?" "What do you think are the countermeasures?" "What do you believe are two or three things you can do to prevent it from happening in the future?" After a brief question-and-answer session, the associate probably will find a solution and fix it himself.

As Al Kinzer, HAM vice-president, explains, "It's as if we ask people to take ownership in what they do here. You don't wait for the next guy to do it. You do it. Management's job is to provide some structure, to administrate, and to encourage people to do well. But most important, management mustn't get in the way. The people in the plant doing their jobs every day are the best ones to handle their problems. A good manager says, I will help you, but I am not going to do it for you. That is your job, and you will figure out the best way to take care of it. *Then* come back to me and I will support your solution.' "

DECISION MAKING BY CONSENSUS

As the term implies, decision making by consensus means a group of people are involved in reaching a resolution. This approach to making decisions isn't unique to Honda; it's a management style used by many organizations.

The process of decision making by consensus accomplishes

two important things: First, it requires involvement during the early stages of planning so several people can provide feedback. The more people who are consulted from different departments, the more likely that there will be a cross-pollination of ideas. Second, by getting people involved, they're more likely to be enthusiastic when their ideas are implemented. People support those things they help to create.

An often-heard complaint expressed by outsiders is that decision making by consensus causes unnecessary delays. A prospective supplier, for instance, may voice this opinion. This, however, is not the case. Important issues receive the highest priority and are acted upon immediately while less important matters wait. What may be essential to a manufacturing company that wants to sell its product to HAM gets tabled or shelved not because decision making by consensus is inefficient but because it is efficient. Well-managed multinational corporations can make important decisions by consensus in short periods of time. At Honda, depending on the urgency, action sometimes is taken instantly. For example, an immediate decision is crucial when a breakdown on the assembly line occurs. The same is true if a shipment of supplies does not arrive on schedule. Other issues are long-term and permit more people to participate in the discussion and planning stages. Honda tries to avoid bogging down good ideas in a bureaucratic shuffle, a fate that frequently dooms promising projects in large organizations.

Shin Ohkubo, an executive vice-president at HAM, says, "When an associate brings an idea to me, even though I may have an opinion, I generally keep it to myself. I'll just listen. Then, following some meetings and reviews of reports to management, I'll express my thinking on the project. But the final decision will be made only as a group. Later, as the manager, I'm held responsible if the project fails. This is what bottoms-up management means to me—it's getting input from associates."

Glenn Barr, who manages HAM's information system department, says, "When our department makes a data processing decision, we bring in people from other departments for their input. By doing this, I've gained considerable knowledge about many areas of the company. By the same token, others learn about data processing." Barr also points out that it's a two-way street. "We're a support department and it's our job to furnish information to various departments to save time for people and make their decision-making process an easy chore. Through the use of our information, we help them meet their objectives and corporate goals."

One drawback of decision making by consensus is that people are required to attend an inordinate number of meetings, sometimes in different departments. Decision making by consensus does not mean that an actual vote is taken and majority rules. Instead, people from different divisions throughout the organization are involved, and if an idea or project has merit, a general agreement will evolve. The level of management that gives approval usually depends on the scope of the project. For example, a costly, long-term objective to build a plant such as HAM was a top management decision, but people at various levels participated in the discussions.

ACCESSIBLE MANAGEMENT

Ever since the publication of the best-selling book, *In Search of Excellence,* the phrase *MBWA* has been quoted in management circles across the country. The authors borrowed it from United Airlines "Management by Walking Around," and Hewlett-Packard's "Management by Wandering Around."

While the physical layout of HAM's open offices makes managers more accessible and eliminate any so-called ivory towers, this does not guarantee associates will approach management with a steady flow of ideas. Nor does it ensure that associates will bring problems into the offices for discussion. Honda managers don't wait for information to pour in from the plant. And they don't depend on their small circle of peers to bring back accurate reports from the plant floor. Instead they go to the production areas to seek out ideas and become familiar with problems firsthand. Honda managers have been practicing what they refer to as "on-the-spot" management ever since the company was founded. As one manager puts it, "We don't discuss theory comfortably sitting behind our desks. We observe firsthand what's going on on the floor in the plant."

All HAM managers spend a significant portion of their day visiting people on the line, eyeball to eyeball. This includes managers from even the most unlikely departments that are the most removed from production—accounting, computer programming, and even legal. Honda Motor chairman, Satoshi Okubo, emphasizes, "We take the realistic and practical approach of observing the actual site, the actual material, and the actual situation. Rather than receiving an explanation about a problem, a manager goes directly to the site to witness it."

An accountant at HAM makes his rounds in the plant. "I have a better understanding of how to classify a machine as an asset after I've seen it," he explains. "My knowledge of equipment also helps to do cost controlling."

All Honda managers in Japan have received some production training. At HAM, practically every manager puts in his or her "line time." It's no different than what McDonald's restaurants refer to as "apron time." The giant fast-food company requires all managers and franchise trainees to spend several weeks behind the grill and to serve customers. Otherwise, they simply wouldn't understand the business. Shelley Lanza, an in-house attorney, put in her time, too. A month after she came aboard at HAM, she spent a week on the line in the welding department. "When there's a maintenance problem in welding," Lanza says, "and I meet with the company and our engineers, I can understand what everyone's talking about." The word got around the plant about her time in the welding department, and it seemed to have a positive effect. Several associates approached Lanza and said, "I give you credit for doing that. It shows how much you really care." Most important, she came across as a real person who was approachable—not as a stiff-shirted attorney in the legal department!

Scott Whitlock, automobile plant manager, confesses that he is one of the few members of the HAM management team who has no production job experience. "Normally, a new person is required to spend some time on the line as part of our training program," he says. "My view is that the associates doing the processes are the real experts. In fact, there's no process in the entire plant where I couldn't find people more qualified than I, so I don't pretend to know it all. However, my legal background seems to work well in my capacity to learn by asking questions. So I do, and by listening attentively to people I am able to do my job effectively. Sure, I depend on everyone else, but then, isn't that an important function of management?"

HAM president Soichiro Irimajiri recalls the time when he was "on loan" to the Ford Motor Company for three months in the 1970s. "I was on an assignment to provide Ford with technical assistance about the CVCC engine. I worked side by side with their engineers, their R&D center, and then I went to the spot—their test lab—to personally observe the tests. To my surprise, there was not a single R&D engineer who also went there to witness the results of the tests, which, incidentally, had many errors. I kept thinking what a difference there is in Ford's management philosophy compared to Honda's."

Irimajiri believes that spending time in the plant is an excellent way for a new manager to get to know people, and likewise, for associates to know the manager. Irimajiri explains how he was able to make the difficult transition from his previous position as executive vice-president of Honda Research and Development to the head of the Suzuka plant, Honda's largest facility. "My first concern was to be able to understand what was happening on the floor. So every morning around five-thirty to six o'clock, I'd come in to talk to associates on the line. I walked around asking a lot of questions, and at first I'm sure nobody even knew who I was. They kept thinking, 'Who is that guy who walks around asking so many questions?' I did that for one year and stayed until nine or ten o'clock at night to catch up with my regular work."

Tetsuo Chino, president of Honda North America, says, "i like to speak directly with people. I don't believe in communicating on paper when there's an opportunity to talk in person." This attitude is far different than what is practiced at so many organizations where memos abound and managers become buried in a sea of minutia. Honda managers prefer to communicate in person because the written word sometimes is misinterpreted.

John Hofmann, manager of the engine plant in Anna, Ohio, claims that he spends as much as 50 percent of his day meeting with people who work on the production line. "Sure, it takes up half my time," Hofmann declares, "but if I didn't do that, I'd be spending even more time attempting to solve problems that occurred because I didn't talk to people. It's a matter of putting the horse in front of the cart instead of behind it."

THE IF PROJECT

The Instruction on Fundamentals (IF) Project is a two-day course with eight hours of films. It addresses the question, "What happens if I don't care about my job or pay attention to quality?" A major portion of the films shows the different processes an automobile goes through as it proceeds from one work station to the next. By viewing work performed by other departments, associates better understand the contributions they make toward the end product, a finished car. They also can see why their work must be done a certain way and how it is coordinated with the next production step. Other films in the IF Project review how HAM production ties in with the marketing organization. The final movie shows enthusiastic reactions of customers.

While the program serves as a refresher course to remind associates about what they previously have been told, it is also a way for the company to express its appreciation for the workers' efforts. One associate said, "The IF Project makes me feel that my link in building each car is vital, and if I break my link, I will break the chain."

THE IDEA CONTEST

Need a good idea for a contest? How about an idea contest?

Honda has one. It's the "Honda World Idea Contest," an

international event for associates that has been held every two years since 1970. What kind of ideas are eligible? All inventions qualify, and not necessarily ones that are work-related or marketable. Past ideas have included a fan-powered bicycle, a motorcycle jacket that warms the rider on cold days with heat from the engine, an expandable car that could seat two to eight people, a bed that throws you out of it if you don't get up on time, a jogging machine on a treadmill that can be maneuvered like a bicycle, a bicycle built for two with riders facing opposite directions, a water roller skate, and snow skis with wheels.

To enter a recent contest, associates at HAM submitted complete descriptions of their ideas on entry forms. From HAM's three plants, thirty ideas were selected from the hundreds submitted, and those contestants were given the funds to build small-scale models. From these thirty, associates voted for two ideas that were built as full-scale working models. The company paid all construction costs. Honda then sent the two facility winners from HAM to Suzuka, Japan to attend the company's World Idea Contest, conducted at the company-owned amusement park and racing circuit, where their winning ideas were presented. The program works in a similar manner at other Honda facilities worldwide.

So far, none of the ideas have been directly marketable, but that's not the purpose of the contest. Its real value is to stimulate associates' imaginations and to encourage bold thinking. When this happens, they also think about ideas that relate to their work.

THE SUGGESTION PROGRAM

The HAM Suggestion Program is much more than a way in which associates can offer their opinions to management. It's a system whereby individuals can change anything about their jobs to improve their work. These ideas range from improving safety conditions to increasing productivity. An associate simply may want to figure out a way to make his or her work easier or less tedious.

Every suggestion is taken seriously. Associates only have to jot their proposed ideas on a single-page suggestion form and submit it to their department manager for review. The response is quick, within forty-eight hours. Management hears every suggestion, even those that are vetoed. Suggestions at HAM are responded to within a day or two. This represents an important difference between Honda's suggestion program and those of other companies. No formal chains of command delay approval, stifle proposals, or discourage participation. "The beauty of our suggestion program is that there's no red tape," says an associate who has submitted several suggestions. "Sometimes a supervisor has let me try things he didn't think would work just so I'd get the experience. There have been times when I'd work between shifts or on a Saturday because I was so anxious to get one of my ideas done. When I worked in a union shop, the foreman wouldn't allow me to touch a tool without permission. And if I did try to fix something on my own, a grievance would be filed on me. It was as if I was being told, 'The company owns the equipment and you can't use it.'"

The Suggestion Program gets people involved because the associates see quick results. During May 1987, for example, 404 suggestions were implemented at HAM. That response translates into 10 percent of the entire plant's work force! People are constantly thinking about ways to improve their work. And the associates on the line are the experts about their work, so they are the people most likely to make improvements in what they do.

Of all suggestions submitted, 59 percent are implemented. (The national average for company suggestion programs is 27 percent.) Although most suggestions represent only minor savings, a step is saved here, and another step there. Those steps can add up.

Sometimes a single suggestion results in the immediate savings of thousands of dollars. The following are a few examples of significant suggestions HAM associates have provided:

Paint filters are made out of a fine steel, and although each costs $25, they were thrown away because they couldn't be cleaned thoroughly. The paint department estimates that more than 200 filters were used each month. Three associates recognized this problem and began experimenting with several different chemical mixtures to effectively clean the filters. After three months of trial and error, in October 1986, they came up with a solvent that was successful. They then designed a container that served as a shaker with the capacity to hold six filters at a time. The entire cleaning process takes only fifteen minutes. The estimated annual savings is $60,000.

In the past, two people (one on each side of the car) were needed to use a hand-held squeeze gun to put a black sealant around the door hinges and fender holes. Two associates, using old parts from discarded robots and combining them with a computer program they devised, developed a new robot. The new robot now does the job, relieving the two associates from the time-consuming and tedious work. Their invention also frees them to do quality checks. The annual savings from this suggestion is $105,000. Soon, other Honda plants also will use these robots, and the savings will be even greater.

The pop-up headlamps on the Accord were a source of frustration because they were difficult to align. During the adjustment process, paint sometimes would chip on the headlamp cowl and the area would have to be repainted. Several staff engineers worked in vain to solve the problem, but it was an associate on the line who came up with a solution. He devised a Plexiglas clip with a millimeter-size index to hold the headlight piece in place after it is painted. The clip does the job and holds it in its position during the alignment procedure. Then, by pulling on the index, the clip easily can be removed. With this suggestion, the chipped paint problem was eliminated. The realized annual savings in labor and materials for using this ten-cent clip is estimated to be $50,000.

Another associate started his career in the automobile welding department in April 1986. About six months later, he began to think about the number of weld tips on the spot-welding robots that had to be replaced every four hours. The associate was told that each tip, which was part of a larger shaft, cost $14.50 and more than sixty were used daily. To save money, he devised a two-piece shaft with a removable tip at its end. Now only the removable tip, which costs $1.79, not the entire shaft, is thrown away. This innovative suggestion saves HAM nearly $200,000 a year, and other Honda plants now are using it. At present, a patent is pending.

Recognition is an essential ingredient in HAM's Suggestion Program. But perhaps the best way to give recognition is HAM president Soichiro Irimajiri's way. Depending on the actual number of suggestions implemented, he devotes two to three days every month to making rounds to each work area and reviewing ideas. During these chats with the president, associates proudly explain and demonstrate what it was that sparked the one special idea about saving time, advancing quality, or improving safety—that one new concept that warrants individual praise from HAM's top executive.

An associate who began his career with Honda on the motorcycle assembly line at age twenty-one, has since advanced to the position of Suggestion Program administrator. While it's impossible to determine the actual number of dollars saved, he estimates the program has generated millions of dollars in genuine savings since its inception in April 1985. "But its monetary value doesn't begin to compare to the stimulating atmosphere it has created. Associates are constantly looking to come up with ideas for improvement," he emphasizes.

The HAM Suggestion Program was "borrowed" from Honda in Japan. Yet it is the Japanese managers who are the most surprised, and most pleased with its success. "They didn't expect our program to be as far advanced as it is until 1990," the manager explains. "During the first year, we patterned ours exactly after theirs, but it wasn't working. So, keeping the same philosophy, we rewrote many of the procedures. Basically we removed the red tape. Apparently the Japanese are a more patient people, and they don't seem to mind waiting for their suggestions to go through the chain of command. On the other hand, our HAM associates want a quicker response. When they have a great idea, they want to do it *now.* Today! So we streamlined the system to accommodate their needs and the program seems to be working outstandingly well now."

At a 1987 seminar in Kansas City, sponsored by the National Association of Suggestion Systems, HAM's program was cited for its effectiveness. Based on the number of suggestions and actual implementations, it was mentioned that the HAM program was perhaps ten to fifteen years ahead of others at major companies in the United States. One major drawback of most programs was that suggestions were presented by workers, but they were implemented by somebody else. "Too frequently, the workers (of other companies) submit an idea and it's the last time they hear about it until they are given an award," a spokesperson for the association explained.

NH CIRCLES

The Now, Next, New Honda Circles program (NH Circles) is more group oriented than the Suggestion Program. An NH Circle is a problem-solving team, usually formed by four or five associates, but the number can be as high as ten. Associates voluntarily band together to devise ways to improve working conditions, quality, safety, and so on. For the most part, NH Circles are formed to solve particular problems, and having accomplished their missions, seek new problems. Some other companies also have what are generally called "quality circles" but most do not. And most do not have specific educational and training programs in place so their employees can follow up on their projects. Without adequate leadership, chaos will undermine the good intentions of a circle's participants.

Quality circles were introduced by an American management consultant, W. Edwards Deming. In the early 1950s, the Japanese Union of Scientists & Engineers invited Deming to present a series of lectures on statistical methods for improving quality on the factory floor. At the time, the Japanese were searching for ways to enhance the image of their goods and increase exports. While many U.S. companies use Deming's teachings, he and another American quality management pioneer, J. M. Juran, are highly acclaimed in Japan for introducing approaches to quality that helped vastly upgrade Japanese products during a twenty-year period.

HAM's own brand of quality circles, NH Circles, is reputed to be the best in the automobile industry in terms of innovation and employee participation. The NH Circle program at HAM is coordinated by Bill Hayes, who began his Honda career in 1981 as a production coordinator in the motorcycle painting department. Hayes had previous paint experience in a supervisory capacity at both Ford Motor Company and Huffy Bicycles, but had no actual administrative background. When he was named to start the project in May 1985, it was both a new assignment and a learning experience for the youthful administrator. Hayes had two major advantages that helped assure the program's success: He could draw from what Honda in Japan had experienced with its quality circles, and he had the HAM associates, who by 1985, were not only a dedicated work force but a seasoned one as well.

Today, while the NH Circle Program is well-organized, complete with training classes, seminars, manuals, and videotapes, Hayes points out that it has few rules and regulations. "Sure, we help develop circles to get them started," he says, "but then they're on their own. We purposely avoid putting parameters on them, because with boundaries, they could become stagnant. We don't want a lot of tight reins on them to take away their creativity."

The company does, however, provide guidance for associates who want to be involved in NH Circle activity, but who aren't sure how to go about it. For instance, direction is given on how to: (1) acquire members for a circle, (2) start the project,

(3) make a plan, (4) choose a theme (mission), (5) set realistic goals, (6) analyze the present situation, (7) break large problems down into small, manageable ones, (8) determine the causes, (9) brainstorm for solutions, (10) try countermeasures, (11) check the results, (12) determine the action, (13) standardize results, and (14) select the next theme.

A significant difference between NH Circles and quality circles of other companies is that at HAM a group can begin a project without prior "approval." The only exceptions are those that require a large investment. All NH Circles give a formal presentation *after* the project has been completed. Many American companies require a presentation *first* as a prerequisite to obtaining authorization.

Twice a year, in March and September, several days are set aside for NH Circle presentations, which are conducted in a packed auditorium. Even vendors make presentations for they, too, have been Honda-inspired and trained by the company to form their own circles. The circles attract a great deal of attention, especially considering that in 1987, nearly one out of three associates was involved in one. The circle members present their projects to a panel consisting of managers that includes top-ranking executives. Many of the presentations are quite elaborate; overhead slide presentations and charts are commonly used; and each circle member has a speaking part. Following a question-and-answer session, audience members make comments and give praise. Each year, the two best circles compete at a worldwide NH Circle Conference in Japan with three associates from each winning circle attending. The competition includes circles from twenty-six different plants and twelve countries.

Each NH Circle is named by its members, who choose colorful names based on the circle's theme, such as Sealer Rats, Mr. Bubble, Final Stage, Hiro's Heroes, and Trail Blazers. Past Circles have included the following.

The Hexagons worked in Material Service and uncrated large steel crates of parts arriving from Japan. With more than 100 bolts per container, as many as 16,000 bolts could end up scattered on the floor by the end of the day! It was a safety and cleanliness problem that ruined the tires of forklift trucks, and was time-consuming to sweep up. The circle's first approach was to invent a spring-loaded clip that would be attached in Japan to each crate. The $3 cost was too high, so that idea was scratched. Somewhat discouraged, the circle regrouped and later devised aprons and magnetic sockets to attach to their airguns, and special bins to collect the bolts. The two shifts conducted a contest to see which could collect the most. Through an investigation, the circle found that the bolts could be sold to a salvaging company for about $1,400 a year. But instead of salvaging the bolts, they decided to recycle them back to Japan to the suppliers. The revenue from recycling the bolts earns an estimated $50,000 a year for the company.

The Suppliers, also a circle in Material Service, consisted of associates who received parts and were required to make copies of each order. Initially, they formed a circle because the copying machine was always breaking down. They also wanted a cart and forklift to ease their work load. After the circle was in progress, its members realized that its original thinking was misguided. They worked on revising the receiving material system for an entire year and ended up making vast improvements in communicating with the purchasing department and the vendors. So, while The Suppliers never did receive a new copying machine, they solved many problems they originally didn't even think about, and in the process, their project generated more than $60,000 in annual savings.

The Cam Washers consisted of associates who worked on the automobile assembly line and installed cam washers on the rear suspensions of the cars. When a cam washer was put on backward, the rear suspension could not be adjusted further down the line. About four or five cars out of 700 per shift needed adjusting, and each required about an hour's worth of labor to fix. The circle came up with a simple but effective solution: A special wrench was developed by welding a small L-shaped bracket on it so if a cam washer was put on backward, the wrench wouldn't tighten it. By doing it this way, an associate simply would reverse the cam washer and install it correctly.

The Work Mates had about seventy seconds to do their jobs while a car was at their assembly line work station. To speed things up, they devised a podium work stand that rearranged their tools in a more organized manner. The result was a reduction in work time of 50 percent. As a result, the Work Mates are reviewing other stations to see whether their idea can be used in other areas of the assembly line.

Many of the NH Circles are ideas that are so obvious that once they have been implemented there's a tendency to ask, "Why hasn't that ever been done before?" But as somebody once said, "Nothing is so uncommon as common sense."

While NH Circle participation is voluntary and takes place after each shift is over, associates do receive overtime wages for partaking in these activities. The extra pay, added to administration costs and material expenses, adds up. In fact, it is estimated that the cost of the program runs over $1 million. But the value attained from the learning process and the teamwork achieved far outweigh the short-term expenses.

THE VOLUNTARY INVOLVEMENT PROGRAM

To serve as a constant reminder to associates to get involved, HAM has a Voluntary Involvement Program (VIP). It's an ongoing merit system that, in part, awards points to associates for their participation and performances in various company activities. Points are given for activity in NH Circles, having perfect attendance, making suggestions, and so on.

VIP points can be converted into a variety of prizes. Associates can receive gift certificates that can be cashed in for Honda merchandise. For outstanding performance over several years they may win a free Honda automobile produced at HAM. For the most part, however, the prizes are by no means lavish; they aren't intended to be. The real reward is not external; it's the feeling one has from knowing he or she has done a good job. Along with their point totals prominently posted near the inside entrance of the plant, the top 100 ranking associates' names and photographs also are displayed. In part, the program's success is a way of keeping score, yet contrary to what may be expected, it doesn't create an environment that pits associates against one another in an effort to gain recognition at the expense of somebody else. This is true because everyone benefits from the program's success. The VIP postings are merely a vehicle for the company to express its gratitude for doing a good job. It also provides an incentive to others, telling them that they, too, should become involved.

10

Two-way Communication: People Speaking Out and People Listening

URING THIS EPOCH OF SPEED, space, and the satellite, communications can be instantly transmitted across millions of miles. But with our ability to transfer information across great distances in microseconds, has our capacity to communicate to another person in the same room increased at all?

In a society where communication has deteriorated between husband and wife, educator and student, and employer and employee, Honda excels in its ability to convey messages and listen to its people. The company has done so in spite of two major obstacles: a language barrier and a home base halfway around the world. It was an awareness of the language barrier that emphasized the need for outstanding communications between the Japanese and Americans. The result is that people speak out and people listen—and messages are conveyed.

Unlike many large organizations, Honda doesn't muddle its channels of communication with a complex and intricate network of managerial levels that confuse and discourage associates from trying to deal directly with high-ranking executives. While the typical Japanese corporation is highly structured and bureaucratic, flexible organizational charts can be found everywhere at Honda.

Because of Honda's flexible organization, effective communication becomes even more critical. A working atmosphere of this nature demands strong leadership. Without close guidance, the company would run under chaotic conditions; constant, consistent communications is the key to getting things done at Honda.

THE "WELCOME ABOARD" MESSAGE

At most companies, it is a rare occasion that a low-level employee has the opportunity to hear or see the company's top-ranking officer. This is not so at HAM. Communications between new associates and top management begin immediately and continue unrestricted. For each new orientation class, usually every week, HAM president Irimajiri delivers an introduction speech to the newest associates.

Irimajiri gives the speech in the plant's auditorium or cafeteria, depending on the group's size. While the speech is, indeed, official, its delivery is quite casual. The plant's top executive is introduced to the new associates as "Mr. Iri." Not knowing what to expect, the audience seems somewhat apprehensive. But the energetic, five-foot-five man quickly puts the people at ease with his sincerity and his convictions. Irimajiri is low-key and soft-spoken, and unlike many other top industrial leaders, his presence is neither threatening nor intimidating. His audience listens intently to his message.

After welcoming the newly hired associates to HAM, Irimajiri explains to his audience that he is not their boss. "Our boss is our customers, and we must never forget that they come first."

He points out that Honda is, and always will be, a technically oriented company. "We have some 10,000 engineers among our 50,000 associates in the world," he says, "and we are spending more than 5 percent of our total revenue on research and development. We have good reason to believe that our technology is superior." He pauses, then adds, "But our technology is not our most important asset. *You* are our most valuable asset. It is up to each of you to perform your best. So I ask you to *think.* Each of you is expected to play an important role in this company. Our success rests on your performances."

A motorcycle and car racing enthusiast, Irimajiri is apt to use many racing analogies during his welcome speech. "Let me tell you about what it takes to be a champion," he tells his audience. "In our racing activities, we must have the best equipment, which, of course, means having the fastest racing car. Second, we need the best driver. Third, we need the best mechanics. Fourth, we need the best engineers. Fifth, we need the best manager. In racing, there are many problems to solve, and only through teamwork can the team become a champion.

"At Honda, we need the best equipment, which, like the racing cars, are our machines. But machinery alone isn't enough. We continually are seeking out the best operators and engineers. *You* people can be the best operators. Likewise, we recruit a major portion of our engineers from our associates on the production line, so some of you may become engineers. And we need the best management people—I hope I can do my best to be one of them."

Irimajiri obviously enjoys talking about competitive racing. He enthusiastically continues: "Let me tell you a story about my personal experience in 1968 when I was working with our Honda team and we were participating in the Grand Prix in Monza, Italy. At the time, we had the most powerful engine with more than 400 horsepower compared to the rest of the field with 360 horsepower. During the race, our driver, Richie Ginther, was able to pass other cars on the front side, but he was losing ground on the back side where the track twisted and curved. After the race, our engineers and mechanics asked, 'Why were you so slow?'

"Ginther, who was obviously upset, replied: 'This machine has some defect.'

"We didn't understand what it could be and were at a loss about how to solve this problem that cost us the race. We knew one existed because our world-class driver told us there was one. Something, obviously, went wrong.

"Later, Ginther asked to have the entire machine taken apart and put on a large table. Then he asked for the suspension to be moved slowly, inch by inch, so we could measure the change of the toe-in. We discovered that it had a 0.002 inch change, and Ginther shouted, 'That's it!'

"Ginther had sensed the trouble might have been the toe-in, but until he actually saw the problem, he could say only, 'I know something is wrong because it doesn't feel right.'

"Nobody accused him of being a poor driver, nor did he point his finger at the mechanics or engineers because they, too, were world-class in their fields. Instead, all members of the team were committed to work together to solve the problem. We knew that, as a team, we could communicate with one another and eventually would come up with a solution. We were willing to put in whatever effort and expenses were necessary because with so many talented people working together, there was no doubt we'd find a solution. The entire team focused on a problem that happened to be two-thousandth of an inch in size. It was the combined effort of the entire group that made the winning difference.

"May I point out that we have problems every day right here in our plant. When a machine is down, nobody says, 'It's your problem, you fix it.' We work together as a team because it is *our* problem.

"As Mr. Honda used to say, 'In a race, a split second can define the entire competition, one tire length will decide whether you are a winner or a loser. If you understand that, you cannot disregard even the smallest improvement.' The same is true in the products we design and build for our customers. So many times the highest efficiency is achieved in design, in manufacturing, in service, by a series of improvements, each one by itself seeming small.

"We are making major improvements in the efficiency in our automobile plant, not from any single big change, but rather from thousands of improvements made by our associates. When added together, they will significantly increase our production efficiency and our competitiveness."

Irimajiri's message is the first of the many times he will communicate directly with these associates.

DAILY MEETINGS—FOR EVERYONE

Never a day passes at HAM when associates don't attend at least one meeting. All associates, for instance, gather in their departments before the shift begins, while team leaders or coordinators conduct informal open-end talks about production schedules, daily goals, the previous shift's problems, and any other subject anybody wishes to discuss. Team leaders also announce new procedures, suggestion program news, and general information about new product models. These meetings last only a few minutes, and provide both inspiration and information. Team leaders encourage associates to ask questions, vent complaints—anything anyone wants to say is welcome.

Sometimes when no major announcements are made, the team leader simply will comment, "You know, for a while it was difficult yesterday, but we managed to take care of our problem and today's a new ball game. You people really did a great job yesterday." Another comment might be, "Yesterday was a bad day for us, and we had to dig our way out of the hole, but now all of that's behind us, so let's see how well we can do today."

During the day, team leaders meet with their coordinators, coordinators meet with department managers, and so on. Communication and information passes in both directions, up and down, throughout the organization.

All managers at HAM attend an early morning production meeting each day in their respective plants. These hour-long conferences are more formal than the shift meetings and generally have a fixed and predictable agenda. Again, everyone is invited to speak out—no subject is too sacred that it can't be brought up for discussion.

Each morning meeting begins with department managers giving accident reports. Safety is such a high priority at HAM that even the most minor injury is reported. It's been said that HAM probably is the only large manufacturer in the United States where top management hears reports on *every* injury, including cuts and bruises.

After the accident reports, the discussion covers the previous day's production numbers, attendance, quality, maintenance, and training reports for each department. General announcements may follow.

Department managers spend a significant portion of their day attending meetings, more so perhaps than managers who work for most other corporations. Their presence is necessary because decisions are made by consensus, so they must be aware of issues even remotely related to their own departments. As one manager says, "Because I'm responsible to be part of the consensus, I need to have a big antenna that keeps reaching out to feed me the right information so I can contribute to the decision-making process."

A common denominator exists at Honda meetings. Regardless of the level of people present, everyone who sits at the table is treated as an equal. It doesn't matter who attends—a secretary, a shop floor associate, a department manager, a senior vice-president—each person is permitted to give his or her input, and most important, each is respected by the group. Before a decision is made, nobody's ideas are considered to be more important than anybody else's. This egalitarianism enhances participation that, in turn, results in open communication. Finally, when the decision is made, everyone moves together in the same direction.

On the surface, a meeting could appear disorganized because anyone who attends can speak out and express his or her opinion. These meetings are not for the timid. Ideas and actions are subject to criticism—and often are. In some ways it resembles a family discussion; when it's all over, a consensus is reached and no ill feelings remain.

SPEAKING "HONDA"

While it is true that most of the Honda Japanese staff transferred to the United States studied English during their formal education in Japan, most have a language problem during their first months here. And only a mere handful of the Americans speak Japanese; the vast majority speak only a dozen or so words. To compensate, graphs and charts are used at practically all meetings. Summary reports rarely are written out without visual displays. This visual communication is sometimes referred to as "speaking Honda."

Many associates say that it takes a while to get used to understanding those Japanese who do speak reasonably good English. "I have to listen very closely," said one associate, "because if I'm not giving my full attention, I simply can't understand what they're saying."

Another associate commented: "Sometimes I have to ask them to repeat what they say several times until it registers. This is embarrassing, and on occasion, it is annoying to both parties."

"It took me a while to realize that when the Japanese nod their heads over and over during a conversation," an American coordinator said, "it doesn't necessarily mean 'yes.' Instead, it means, 'I understand what you're saying' rather than giving an affirmative reply."

"While the language differences were a severe problem when the motorcycle plant first began production," an executive vice-president explains, "it actually served to our advantage when we first started training associates at HAM. This is true because a trainer was forced to take every step himself, and then let the associate do it. The process was repeated until the associate was able to do everything on his or her own."

One associate says, "Kids play 'show and tell' in school. At Honda, we practice 'show and *do.*' Actually, teaching somebody how to work on an assembly line involves more showing than telling, and with the language barrier that existed between the Japanese and Americans, we automatically became more attentive to what they did. In retrospect, we probably learned more this way."

Susan Insley, HAM's vice-president of corporate planning, acknowledges that the language problem creates a communication awareness. "It forces everyone to try harder," she emphasizes. You have to *think* before you speak, and you must speak more carefully and succinctly. By crystalizing your thoughts to make certain that people understand, your message gets through to the other party."

THE SPEAK-OUT PROGRAM

The Speak-out Program serves as an avenue for airing complaints, voicing opinions, and demanding answers to questions. Unlike the Suggestion Program, it does not promote involvement, but instead provides feedback about what associates are thinking. In short, it encourages them to express their gripes. Completing the program's one-page form is the surest way for an associate to be heard. The form only has to be deposited in any of the twenty or so mailboxes throughout the plant. A copy also is given to either the associate's team leader or to the coordinator, and a response is guaranteed within forty-eight hours.

Because two or more people review the form, more than one reaction will result. And what one person thinks is a poor idea may be viewed by another as having merit. Then, too, knowing that somebody else also will pass judgment makes both parties consider it seriously.

Suggestion systems are not unique to Honda. In fact, a multitude of suggestion boxes can be found in manufacturing plants throughout the United States. For the most part, however, they serve only as a vain reminder of the lack of communication within a particular organization. Programs of this nature work only when proper follow-up is executed. A HAM personnel manager says, "We make sure that a quick response always is dispatched. This is what makes it work. Every associate *knows* that by dropping the form into that little box, it's a certainty that a reply will follow. It's like sending a package via Federal Express. You know it is going to be received at the other end. Only when people have confidence in a program of this nature will they use it."

THE WAIGAYA

Waigaya is a Japanese word that means chattering. But the Honda definition has come to be a meeting of a group of people where everyone can freely express his or her opinion. During one of these open forums, everyone is encouraged to speak freely, and often, two or more people are talking at the same time. Hence there is much chattering.

Another unusual characteristic of a waigaya is that the participants express whatever is on their minds. Their thoughts don't have to focus in on any particular subject. People are welcome to talk about their dreams concerning how they envision the Honda of tomorrow. The discussion of any subject is permissible.

Waigayas are somewhat like brainstorming sessions and are regularly conducted at all levels throughout the Honda organization. A waigaya can include associates and managers from many departments, thereby making it possible to consolidate the thinking from two or more sections of the company. For instance, marketing people, designers, and engineers may attend a waigaya. Honda is unique among Japanese auto makers in that the free flow of ideas exists between a cross section of company employees and specialists who congregate to express different views. One reason these informal meetings work is that no regard is given to one's rank.

The concept of waigaya was introduced to Honda in 1973 by today's chairman of the board, Satoshi Okubo, while he was a managing director of the company. "When the company was small, our founder, Mr. Honda, was not a person who would bring out ideas within a team," Okubo explains. "Although he was a genius who served as an inspiration to others, he was a man who did things his own way. So a waigaya is an avenue through which a group of nongenius people can use their collective brainpower to express their dreams and desires to produce new ideas and concepts. We felt it was important to have these sessions as the company grew in size to maintain an open forum where people feel comfortable expressing their opinions. When we first had these sessions, we didn't call them by any specific name. The name 'waigaya' just evolved, and to my knowledge no other company uses this term."

A waigaya can range from an informal meeting over lunch to a formally organized top-level management session, such as the two that are held each year at retreats in Japan. These semiannual waigayas include the eight top senior managers of the company and last for a few days. Another annual one-day waigaya includes the company president, chairman of the board, and the executive vice-president. The company's managing directors also attend a half dozen or so official waigayas that are held away from the company headquarters in a relaxed atmosphere. Some waigayas have specific agendas, while others are more loosely conducted around a general topic.

But most often, waigayas occur at lower levels throughout every area of the company. What makes a waigaya so important to Honda's decision-making process is that ideas are discussed and developed in great detail. Unlike brainstorming, where all ideas and suggestions are considered for discussion, in a waigaya ideas may be challenged and rejected by the group, quickly honing a project or an idea to its completion.

11

Quality, Efficiency, and Productivity

WHEN the first Accord models rolled off the HAM assembly line in November 1982, the skeptics' faces blushed red. Honda had demonstrated that the American worker could produce high-quality cars as well as the Japanese. Independent car experts scrutinized the new models and lauded their automotive excellence. Nonbelievers soon became believers as demand for the cars soared and plant operations increased to full capacity, where they have remained ever since. In explaining the new factory's success, one industry expert said, "The factory is simply better organized and more efficiently run than the plants of the domestic auto makers."

Compare HAM to a well-operated traditional plant. In 1986, 3,000 HAM associates produced 1,330 cars daily in a $500 million plant. In contrast, General Motor's much-touted, $600 million Hamtramck plant in Detroit was producing 960 cars with a work force of 5,800. The Honda plant used about 2 million square feet, including an area for stamping all metal body panels and a place for the plastic injection molding that produced instrument panels and bumper covers. The GM plant used almost 3 million square feet and its stamping and plastic molding were done elsewhere.

GM officials boasted that its state-of-the-art Hamtramck plant was well equipped with sophisticated robots and automation. While HAM's automated welding shop probably is the most sophisticated in the automobile industry, overall the plant does not rely heavily on robotics. The difference is that fewer HAM associates are capable of producing more. That's called productivity.

Yet, if the HAM associates had been unable to match the quality of the Japanese-made Hondas, there would be no success story to tell today. If the HAM production had been judged as inferior, the demand for all Honda cars, including its imported models, would have dropped dramatically.

MONITORING QUALITY CONTROL

Honda's success does not come from doing a single thing many times better, but from doing many things a little better. Certainly, many of its management techniques are not unique; the company has exercised good judgment in "borrowing" many concepts from the outside. Honda borrowed one such concept from quality guru, W. Edwards Deming, the American consultant whom the Japanese revere for introducing statistical process control to Japanese manufacturers.

In 1963, less than two years after he had graduated from Waseda University's engineering school, Honda Motor Company chose Shin Ohkubo, now executive vice-president of HAM, to attend classes for five months to study Deming's methods. The twenty-four-year-old engineer had to study methods to upgrade the factory's production quality, then teach it to others, who would introduce it to still others within the Honda organization. After Ohkubo digested the information, he worked with a team of six associates who inspected motorcycle parts, found hundreds of defects, and subsequently established a system to document what they uncovered. The Ohkubo team's purpose was to reveal potential problems, adjust processes, and develop a system. A sophisticated statistical analysis was needed to monitor the maze of intertwining relationships. Then the team identified each problem that led to poor quality. For the next two years, Ohkubo taught quality control principles to many Honda associates.

Ohkubo explains, "Quality is achieved through the combination of good materials, equipment, and experienced people who are dedicated to their jobs. When all of those elements are brought together correctly and are in harmony with each other, high quality is going to be achieved.

"But one must realize that there always will be variations in the material and the machine. In fact, the most experienced person's work can fluctuate. In many ways, a machine operator can be compared to a golfer. Golf balls are a standard material, and the club, like the machine, is basically the same. But a golfer never has the exact same stroke, and similarly, a machine operator's work varies. It is for this reason that Honda managers go to the spot on the factory floor to have direct contact with an actual operation. It's not possible to analyze and control quality from behind a desk any more than a golf swing can be corrected by a teaching pro who isn't out on the course. The manager, like the golf pro, must observe all variations so he or she can determine what adjustments are needed to achieve top performance."

A PRODUCTIVE WORK FORCE

While preparing a feasibility study on building a U.S. plant, Honda commissioned an American labor expert to assist with the research. During a tour of the Saitama factory, the consultant observed an "interesting phenomenon." When a chime rang to signify the beginning of a ten-minute break, many of the production associates continued working for an extra thirty to fifty seconds. Even typists continued to work an extra thirty to fifty seconds after the bell, finishing perhaps a paragraph or a page before taking their breaks. Only then did people go outside and sit on the lawn, smoke a cigarette, or drink a beverage.

The labor expert believed the thirty- to fifty-second delay was significant because associates received only two ten-minute breaks each day.

"No big deal," Honda managers told him. "This is common at all of our plants."

"In America, this never would happen," the expert commented, "so don't expect it there. At the sound of the bell, American workers drop everything and will *run,* not walk, to the nearest exit. I've seen typists stop typing in the middle of a sentence."

But it did happen in America. At HAM, associates appear to possess the same commitment as those Honda associates in Japan. For the most part, it has to do with the way associates are treated at HAM. When people are treated with respect and have pride in their work, they are more conscientious about their performance. To the skeptic, this sounds somewhat simplistic, but the proof is the fact that HAM's associates are considered one of the most productive work forces in the world.

While a few seconds doesn't seem like a big deal, the time can add up. In a 1986 survey by Robert Half International, a recruiting consultant, American workers "steal" an average of four hours and twenty-nine minutes a week, which equals six weeks a year. In the study, the firm defined theft as the "deliberate and persistent abuse of job time." Examples of how employees cheat companies include: habitually arriving late or leaving early, pretending to be ill, using company property and time to take care of personal business, taking long lunch hours and coffee breaks, and creating the need for overtime by working slowly.

Half said that about $197 billion worth of all U.S. employers' time each year is stolen—an amount equal to the entire American automobile industry's sales!

LITTLE STEPS GO A LONG WAY

An ancient Oriental proverb says that each long journey is made one small step at a time. At Honda, little steps are regarded as integral parts of the total manufacturing process. Associates are continually reminded to seek new ways to improve productivity. It is these small contributions made on a day-in and day-out basis by all associates that ultimately make a big difference.

On several occasions throughout the year, HAM associates hear President Irimajiri remind them of the strong competition that the company faces in the world marketplace. He points out how the unfavorable exchange rate has a direct bearing on Honda and how other auto makers all over the world are increasing their manufacturing capacities. In his speeches, Irimajiri is apt to make reference to the two kinds of resources that the plant must rely on to increase productivity in order to maintain its competitive edge. "There are the hard resources that consist of such things as machinery and buildings," he states, "and there are soft, or human resources. It is each of you whom we depend on to find ways to save time and reduce effort at your daily jobs. Think of ways that you can save small steps to increase productivity. If everyone can save an extra second here, and another here, tens of thousands of savings of seconds will be realized day after day."

Associates are told that just a single second saved by each of them collectively totals more than 4,000 seconds, or over a full hour a day. That extra hour, during the course of a year, translates into many extra automobiles. Seconds do matter.

Irimajiri's message is clear: Increased productivity is not necessarily achieved by speeding up the production line, working harder, adding on new plant space, or purchasing more equipment such as robots to reduce manhours. The entire plant can become more productive by using and streamlining each process performed by each associate. It's up to everyone to think about new ways to implement savings. While each single step saved may seem insignificant, the total combined savings realized by the entire work force is monumental.

JUST-IN-TIME PRODUCTION

Honda plants carry parts sufficient for a few production hours or a few production days. In fact, vendors in Ohio and nearby states often ship parts to HAM every few hours. These arrive at the plant and are moved to the production line just in time. HAM keeps parts from faraway vendors, such as those in California and Japan, in three-day inventories.

Honda achieves a high degree of efficiency with its version of the Just-in-Time (JIT) system, which other well-run Japanese—and now American—companies have been using for years. JIT production arose from the severe Japanese land shortage. Initially, JIT provided a way to move parts to the production line in a short time, which reduced the need for storage space. In the United States, space always has been available, so the need for JIT never has been a pressing issue. But the system recently has revealed some excellent economic and quality advantages, and today more and more American businesses are beginning to incorporate the JIT system.

When properly done, both the manufacturer and the parts vendor can carry low inventories. As one HAM purchasing manager explains: "We don't want a vendor keeping a high inventory either because eventually he'll pass the cost on to us."

One Honda manager compares JIT to a ship steaming down a river. When the water level is high, the captain is not concerned about the river's bottom. But when the water level is low, the captain must carefully watch for the rocks and reefs at the river's floor. And workers and engineers in a manufacturing plant also run a tighter, more conscientious ship when the inventory level is low. JIT is designed to expose problems instead of concealing them. The system promotes efficiency because it forces people to find and solve problems early so that disturbances are avoided altogether. In the long run, the company saves money because it has less downtime and fewer expensive repairs.

REPAIRING AND MAINTAINING MACHINES

Just as outstanding service is essential to selling, repairing and maintaining machinery is essential to a manufacturing plant's efficiency. Poorly repaired or improperly maintained equipment can produce bad parts or cause the production line to shut down altogether.

In the case of a minor malfunction, the production associate who operates a machine probably will fix it, because he or she not only knows the equipment but has the skills to do so. It goes back to the Honda philosophy that emphasizes "nobody knows the job better than the person who does the actual work."

Of course, not every associate can correct every malfunction—some mechanical breakdowns require an expert. Here's where Honda's pride in being neither a motorcycle nor an automobile company, but an *engineering firm,* comes into effect. With about 20 percent of its 58,000 or so employees being engineers or R&D associates, there always will be people in the plant who are able to fix just about anything that can go wrong with a machine. In the rare event that no one within HAM can handle the problem, the company will fly in an expert from anywhere in the world within twenty-four hours to correct the situation. The expert, for example, may work with the machine's manufacturer, or the expert may be an individual or team of people from Japan. From Tokyo it is a twelve-hour, nonstop flight to Detroit, followed by another forty-minute flight to Columbus, so bringing an expert from Japan could take a full working day. Time is always of the essence when anything goes wrong that could affect production at HAM. Whoever can fix the problem will be brought in from anywhere.

In the beginning when a catastrophic breakdown occurred, HAM had to rely on experts from its parent company, a Japanese manufacturer, or a specialist from Honda's wholly owned subsidiary, Honda Engineering Company Ltd., which designs and builds a high percentage of the company's major machines. In addition to making machines, Honda's in-house machine-tool builder integrates the machines into the plant's flow. Today, however, a staff of competent engineers is available at the U.S. Honda Engineering, which is headquartered at the auto plant site just down the road from HAM, so a problem rarely requires bringing in someone from Japan. While Honda

Engineering in Japan has a work force of thousands, Honda expects to employ 200 or so at its U.S. engineering division by 1991.

While breakdowns never will be eliminated, proper maintenance certainly can prevent many problems. At 5:00 A.M. each workday, ninety minutes before the first shift begins, the three dozen or so members of a preproduction crew known as HAM Facilities Engineering and Maintenance begins work. The group coordinator proudly says, "We are a part of production." He justifies his statement by explaining, "For instance, if the chilled water system lost even 20 percent of its capacity every department would be affected. In areas like the paint department, it could shut down the entire production line."

In addition to the water system, this department oversees such functions as electricity, steam and air power, water and waste treatment, fuel supplies, and construction. The challenge of keeping more than 2 million square feet maintained at a constant temperature of 78°F is, by itself, quite a task. Humidity must be kept low because, besides affecting the working conditions, it can have disastrous effects on the paint. The sheer size of HAM creates a monumental maintenance job. For instance, the plant produces enough air conditioning each summer day to cool 3,200 homes. In the winter, it produces enough heat for 7,000 homes, or a community of 21,000 people. Each year, it consumes 162 billion watt-hours of electricity, enough for 12,000 homes, or a town with 36,000 people. And 1.2 million gallons of industrial and sanitary waste are disposed daily.

To help approach the goal of zero defects, Facilities Engineering and Maintenance has a computer system that runs routine maintenance checks on parts and equipment for every machine in the plant. With these devices, the team can predict when certain machines are about to break down.

THE PACIFIC IS A TWO-WAY OCEAN

While this chapter has focused on the manufacturing end of the business, the fascinating story behind Honda International

Trading Corporation (HIT) demonstrates the constant company-wide emphasis on efficiency.

In September 1972, purchasing manager Shige Yoshida was sent to the United States to buy auto parts and raw materials. About two and a half months later, Yoshida told Honda's general manager of purchasing that his search for goods had been unsuccessful because "things in America were too expensive, particularly after transportation costs were added."

But instead of being instructed to return to Tokyo, Yoshida was told, "We are happy to report to you that you have a permanent assignment with American Honda. We want you to continue your search." So Yoshida began buying samples of parts and materials, which he shipped to Japan for evaluation. A federal law offering tax benefits to domestic corporations that export 95 percent or more of their sales prompted Honda to form its subsidiary company, HIT.

In the beginning, the goods sent to Japan were minor compared to Honda products shipped to the United States. At first, HIT took the "easy route" and sent products such as bath towels and golf balls to be sold to Honda employees. The first year sales totaled a meager $50,000. Later, the trading company became more ambitious and exported a variety of merchandise to Japan. As its shipping requirements grew, Honda began to purchase its own cargo ships, and today it owns five. Honda's ongoing objective of achieving efficiency is illustrated by its efforts to fill the cargo ships that bring cars from Japan and not let them return empty. In 1987, its exports were approximately $150 million.

The subsidiary ranks among the leading exporters of U.S. goods to Japan in five of its product lines: third in aluminum scrap, eighth in aluminum ingots, first in waste paper, second in alfalfa hay cubes, and first in live beef cattle. True to founder Soichiro Honda's constant effort for efficiency as well as cleanliness, the cattle pens are hospital clean. Special pens are used to decrease the cattle's movement during the long ocean voyage in order to reduce their amount of weight loss. Its lists also includes Original Equipment Manufacturer (OEM) exports, such as generator and lawn mower parts, auto seat fabrics, headlights, and catalytic converters.

Honda's 1990 export target to Japan is for a minimum of $1 billion. While the U.S. trade deficit climbs higher and higher, HIT is helping to make the Pacific a two-way ocean.

12

Long-term Relationships

O N ITS BALANCE SHEET, an automobile manufacturing company's assets are top-heavy with buildings, land, machinery, equipment, cash, receivables, and, of course, vast inventories. While no ledger entry places a value on human resources, people are, indeed, Honda's most valuable assets.

Since Honda's inception, Soichiro Honda has emphasized that people are the most important factor in determining his young enterprise's ultimate success. The founder espoused:

> You have to act as if everyone around you is a guest, a customer, and that will affect the product. People talk about innovation, but it doesn't just happen. If you think people are important and you want to improve their lives, that's when innovation occurs.

His thoughts permeated the entire organization then as well as now. *People,* not inventions or machines, are the cornerstone upon which the Honda Motor Company has been built.

RECRUITING— THE SELECTION PROCESS

When HAM announced it would be hiring people to work at its Ohio motorcycle plant, it stirred a lot of excitement in Union County. After all, this rural farming community had little industry, and the opening of a $35 million factory meant new jobs would soon be available.

In 1978, few local residents had the slightest notion that about a decade later, two automobile plants would adjoin the motorcycle factory. Nor could anyone imagine that employment would skyrocket to more than 5,200 by 1987 and be projected to hit 8,650 by 1991. Honda's capital investment in Ohio will rise to nearly $1.7 billion by 1990.

In the beginning, there was strong public opinion in Union County that Honda's attempt to manufacture quality motorcycles would fail, that the local labor pool simply could not produce motorcycles at the same level as the Japanese. But to the unemployed Union County workers, a job was a job, and even a temporary job would put some food on the table.

Honda, however, never had any intention of hiring temporary workers. The company had long-term plans. The first task was to recruit the best available people within a thirty-mile radius.

While HAM does not have a lifetime employment policy like Japanese Honda and like many other companies in Japan, its recruiters sought people for long-term employment. Accepting personnel turnover is a poor way to conduct business; it is both costly and demoralizing. To keep turnover to a minimum and to assure high-quality workmanship, Honda's recruiting approach calls for carefully hand-picking each associate after extensive interviews. In this respect, HAM selects its people differently from other major Japanese auto makers, and for that matter, even its sister plants in Japan. In Japan, job applicants take lengthy examinations as the first step of a long procedure to secure employment.

In fact, it is routine for other Japanese auto makers to administer employment tests in the United States. At its Georgetown, Kentucky, plant, Toyota subjects recruits to rigorous examinations. It is not unusual for a recruit to spend as many as twenty-five hours proving himself or herself to the Japanese auto maker. The rigorous screening includes paper-and-pencil tests, workplace simulations, and a probing interview. There are also mock production lines where applicants assemble tubes or circuit boards. The purpose is to identify applicants who can keep a fast pace, endure tedious repetition, and yet stay alert. The tube-assembly procedure is intentionally flawed and applicants are asked how they would improve it. Not only literacy and technical knowledge are examined but also more subjective things like interpersonal skills.

Extensive testing is also standard procedure at Mazda's plant in Flat Rock, Michigan. At its Smyrna, Tennessee, plant, Nissan prefers to give probable hires at least forty hours of "preemployment" training—without pay. The training is intended partly as a final check on whether the company and those in training are right for each other.

Instead of testing prospective associates with written examinations, HAM conducts three separate interviews, during which Honda executives and recruiters probe for clues indicating applicants' attitudes toward work. The interviews reflect the importance the company places on personal relationships. HAM managers believe written exams are both sterile and impersonal and therefore constitute a poor beginning for the close relationship the company wants to establish with potential associates.

Conducting extensive interviews is a painstaking task, but a necessary part of Honda's constant quest for quality. The first interview is conducted with one to five interviewees (the group interview is relatively new and designed to decrease the tens of thousands of hours spent on recruiting each year). Those applicants called back are individually interviewed by two managers, and if invited back a third time, again are questioned by at least two interviewers. Depending on the position available, an interviewee might meet with a panel of HAM managers. The third meeting is considerably longer than the earlier ones, often running for several hours. All in all, it is a time-consuming effort compared to how other companies weed out large numbers of people through written examinations before the interviews. "While it would save a lot of time if we distributed written tests to a room full of applicants in our cafeteria and then interviewed only the ones with high scores, we don't believe in treating people like cattle," says one

HAM manager. "So we do it the hard way, eyeball to eyeball."

Landing a job at Honda has turned out to be more difficult than many central Ohio people imagined. Those who applied for the first jobs at HAM quickly discovered that it wasn't simply a matter of writing down what work they had done before or having an "in" with somebody at the plant. At HAM, it was different—having somebody inside to put in a good word was no guarantee for employment.

The vast majority of associates employed at HAM today had little or no prior manufacturing experience. Furthermore, there were no automobile or motorcycle manufacturers in the vicinity, so few people knew how to build the products. Al Kinzer, HAM's vice-president, claims that this actually worked as an advantage because "we didn't want people to start with bad habits. In many cases, birth is easier than resurrection. When you have never built an automobile, then you probably will accept our high standards for doing the job."

There are many stories about unlikely candidates with diverse backgrounds who went on to succeed as productive HAM associates. This list includes a former pig farmer, the son of a grain mill operator, a divorcée with four small children, and a vocational school teacher. The nature of jobs previously held is not nearly as important as one's attitude about work. The number one objective of the interviews is to determine, before they are hired, how well people will do as HAM associates.

Honda can afford to be particular. In 1986, HAM received 14,700 applications. The company hired 1,400 workers, making it as tough to get a job there as to get into an Ivy League college. At the end of 1987, Honda had more than 25,000 applications on file. And at Honda Power Equipment in Swepsonville, North Carolina, 4,000 people applied for 100 jobs.

Many of the HAM interview questions focus on determining if an individual will be a "good fit" in the company. "We're looking for team players, not superstars," Kinzer explains. "We want a bunch of .290 hitters. After all, a team rarely needs a .600 hitter, if it has all of those steady .290 guys constantly working to meet its objectives. And if everyone on the team bats .290, I guarantee you that the team will be a winner."

The questions will vary from interviewer to interviewer, but with enough answers, HAM can form a profile of each job seeker to determine his or her qualifications. The following are a cross-section of questions likely to be asked during an interview:

> Do you maintain your own car or motorcycle?
> What are your short-term and long-term goals in life?
> What are you looking for in an employer?
> Why do you want to work for Honda?
> What is the best thing and the worst thing you've ever heard about Honda?
> If you were offered two jobs at the same pay and with the same benefits, what else would you consider to determine which company to work for?
> If you were working on the assembly line and couldn't keep up with it, what would you do?
> If somebody who had worked on the assembly line for five years kept passing you bad parts, what would you do?
> What would be your reaction if you were hired by Honda, but not assigned to any work in your specialized field?
> In what areas are you most creative?
> Do you share your ideas with others?
> What is your definition of teamwork?
> What do you believe are some of the advantages and disadvantages of teamwork in the workplace?
> What is your average work week?
> How do you feel about working 50 hours a week?
> Will long hours present a problem to your family?

One of the secrets for conducting an effective interview is that the interviewer must be a good listener. Honda recruiters recognize the importance of finding out what the interviewee thinks. Yes, in-depth recruiting is an expensive and time-consuming process. But when people are a company's most valuable asset, hiring is not the place to economize. HAM's recruiting objective is to attract the best available people and the plant's future depends on how well this objective is met.

In addition to question-and-answer sessions, applications and résumés are carefully reviewed. Background information, from tardiness to a high employment turnover, is discussed. HAM has enjoyed a continuous program expansion since its opening, so it is not uncommon for associates to find themselves transferred to different positions. For this reason, flexibility is a key element; an electrical engineer might be placed in an entirely different line of work at a future date, as might a welder, an accountant, or a secretary.

An interview is effective when it is a two-way street; this means that applicants must be encouraged to ask questions, and ample time is set aside so company philosophies and attitudes can be explained fully. Honda recruiters don't hesitate to tell it like it is. As one manager explains, "If somebody doesn't feel comfortable with our work environment, like the open office concept, wearing a uniform, and the lack of private parking spaces, then he or she probably won't fit in at HAM."

Another manager states: "We try to discourage 4:01-ers, guys who rush out of the place at exactly one minute after quitting time. We also let people know that they might be asked to put in some overtime now and then. We try to be up front with everyone so there won't be any surprises later on. If a person isn't going to be happy here, there's no point in coming to work here."

HAM's nepotism rule does not permit members of the same family to work at the plant—for an unusual reason: Honda has a commitment to serve the entire community. By eliminating the employment of spouses and children of the same household, more families are able to become involved with the company.

PROMOTING PEOPLE

The key is to put good people on the payroll, and then make sure they are properly trained and developed. If not, even the best recruiting efforts are wasted.

Throughout this book, it has been documented that Honda devotes considerable dollars and energy toward developing people. Witness, for instance, HAM's willingness to send associates to Japan to be taught and updated on the latest manufacturing techniques. Similarly, there is the continuous effort to develop sales and service people at the dealer level.

Investing in people has paid off. Honda's employment turnover is slightly more than 2 percent—minuscule compared to domestic automobile companies. HAM's job rotation program, for example, develops several skills to avoid obsoleteness due to changes in technology. Bringing young, promising associates in during the early stages of long-term projects allows the associates to participate in their own futures. When decisions are made by consensus, people feel they have a vested interest in their company's future.

Honda promotes people from within, whereas other manufacturers recruit managers from other companies. When outsiders are chosen over long-term employees, morale is crushed; people think that no matter how hard they work to prove themselves worthy for advancement, it doesn't really matter to management. A work force's morale is significantly dependent on its right to earn advancement. Of course, an obvious advantage to promoting from within is that managers who have worked their way to the top are personally familiar with what goes on at various work stations on the plant floor. And most important, they know many people within the organization. A close look at Honda reveals that throughout the organization, the vast majority of senior management began careers with the company at entry level positions. As one HAM manager points out, "It's a sign of failure when a company must appoint outsiders to top positions."

THE VENDORS

A major portion of an automobile's contents is manufactured by outside companies, commonly referred to as vendors. Like other auto makers, Honda does business with several hundred vendors, and here too, long-term relationships play a vital role. Vendors are frequently referred to as Honda's "business partners," and as in the plant itself, teamwork is a key element in determining the success of these ventures.

For obvious reasons, the quality of the products manufactured by these companies has a direct bearing on the quality of each car that rolls off HAM's assembly line. As HAM president Shoichiro Irimajiri says: "When we look to suppliers, we seek companies that believe in the same things we do because they are not selling their products merely to Honda, they are selling their products to our customers, through Honda." In 1986, Honda bought more than $641 million in parts and materials from more than 400 American vendors. In 1987, that increased more than $935 million. Honda's high standards of workmanship can be only as good as the sum total of those parts received from its vendors.

Selecting vendors is an ongoing effort conducted by the research group, a division of Honda's purchasing department. When the purchasing department recently placed an ad in a trade magazine announcing it wanted to find a source of more small stamped and welded parts in the United States, more than 200 companies replied. Each received an extensive application. After evaluating the responses, potential vendors were invited to HAM for formal interviews. The visitors toured the plant, met with HAM associates, and were encouraged to ask questions. Then Quality Assurance Visits (QAVs) were scheduled where members of the research team inspected each potential supplier's plant.

During a series of QAVs, each plant is meticulously scrutinized. Everything from the plant's cleanliness to its quality standards is reviewed. HAM officials question financial stability, maximum production capacity, and quality consistency. After the initial visit, HAM's purchasing department identifies any shortcomings. The findings are discussed with the supplier, who must implement certain changes within a given time period to remain a contender. Later, after certain qualifications have been met, HAM will request that quotes be submitted on a specific item the supplier is deemed capable of producing.

Another facet of the evaluation process involves the development of a sample part, which is thoroughly studied by Honda R&D North America. During this phase, the sample parts are put through a series of tests, including durability, corrosion resistance, and functionality.

To be competitive in the marketplace, Honda must negotiate reasonable prices with those companies that supply parts for its automobiles. But getting the best price is by no means the highest priority. As a matter of policy Honda attempts to secure contracts that assure a decent profit for the vendor. As one purchasing manager says, "We don't want to enter a relationship with people by squeezing them so tight that they're forced out of business. We recognize that suppliers have a substantial investment in their capital equipment, and it's necessary for them to get a good return or they'll go belly up. We're interested in establishing long-term relationships with our vendors."

Traditionally, a manufacturing company's purchasing agent is instructed to get three quotes, take the lowest, and execute an order. Honda insists on a detailed breakdown of each quotation. Included are the prices for such things as raw materials, fabrication, packaging, and transportation. Through this disclosure, Honda may identify certain problems and thereby assist the bidder in becoming more efficient. While the decision making is a thorough and time-consuming process, once it is made the implementation is much quicker than the norm. One vendor says, "With most companies, it's just the opposite. Even though they accept a bid, it takes a long time before the actual order is processed and a shipment is made."

Unlike some auto makers, Honda doesn't mind working with vendors that also supply parts to Honda's competition. In fact, diversification sometimes is encouraged for the sake of good business. Honda does, however, frown on a vendor's receiving a large percentage of its total business from another auto maker because the other company may exert too much control. Honda wants to be an important customer, entitled to special attention.

In addition to carefully screening vendors, Honda has a grading system it uses *after* the contract is signed. Quality grade cards are forwarded monthly to vendors. These reports inform each vendor of its score, and failure to perform in compliance with Honda's rigid standards could lead to the reduction or elimination of future orders. One vendor said his company recently sent 316,000 parts to HAM, and a grade card indicated that 44 parts had been rejected. Although he was told that the report was satisfactory, it was not outstanding. "I thought we did a good job," he states, "but Honda wants us to do even better—so we will."

About 60 percent of the 1988 HAM models were made with American components. This figure is expected to increase to 67 percent in 1989, and rise to 75 percent in 1991. As the company establishes good working relationships with domestic vendors, its dependence on Japanese imports will steadily decline. Since production first began at HAM, Honda's first priority has been to buy parts from U.S. vendors, but never at the expense of quality. Initially American suppliers either were unwilling or unable to make the necessary changes to comply with Honda's specifications. To do so entailed massive capital outlays for R&D, tooling and production changes, conversion to the metric system, shortening of lead times, improvement of quality control, and so forth.

Honda's second preference is a joint venture that would merge the technologies and know-hows of two capable companies. In such a case, a collaboration agreement is executed between an American company and a Japanese vendor that has a good track record with Honda.

Third, Honda will work with a highly regarded Japanese supplier that opens a U.S. factory. As one HAM purchasing manager explains, "When given a choice, we prefer to buy from American suppliers, but our survival depends on our ability to purchase the best available parts, and in this regard it doesn't matter if they're European, Japanese, American, or Martian!"

A fourth option is for Honda to manufacture an item in-house or through a joint venture with another company—either Japanese or American.

The final option is to import parts from Japan until one of the four choices above becomes feasible. For instance, a superior specialty steel that the company uses today for body panels originally was unavailable in the United States. While these panels were being imported from Japan, Honda engineers were working diligently with an American steel manufacturer to develop the technology. As a result, all auto body parts made at HAM today use only American steel; no other U.S. auto maker can make this claim. With the exception of one specially treated steel that is used to form the Gold Wing motorcycle gas tanks, all motorcycle steel is also produced in this country. At present this unusual steel is unavailable in America, and it is anticipated that, in a matter of time, a U.S. supplier will also produce this steel.

An Inland Steel manufacturer stated at the 1987 U.S. International Trade Commission: "At the beginning, Inland Steel Company could not meet Honda's technical and quality requirements. But Honda committed to work with us as a partner to solve these problems. Specifically, Honda's and Inland Steel's engineers and production people worked closely to determine what needed to be done to meet the requirements by cooperating with Nippon Steel Company, Honda's major supplier in Japan."

In Armco's 1986 annual report, a statement read:

> In the early 1980s when Honda first began building cars in the United States, we tried to become a supplier, but we didn't make it. But we didn't give up. As our quality improved and we refocused on the customer; we returned to Honda, not to become a supplier, but rather a partner.

Randall Clark, president of Dunlop Tire, which made 100 percent of the tires for 1987 U.S. Civics—the company's first OEM relationship with a U.S. auto maker—explains how his company worked closely with Honda to establish a strong relationship: "We put together a team to go to the Marysville factory to correlate our data with Honda's statistical data, to work closely on the shop floor with the Honda people. That interchange was critical to the process by which we can build a world-class product for a world-class company."

Obviously, it helps for the American manufacturer to be persistent. When an American jack company attempted to sell its wares to HAM in 1985, it was politely informed that its product did not meet Honda's quality standards. The company asked to study Honda's jack specifications, but the request was denied, so it did what Japanese companies do in similar situations: It bought a Honda jack, analyzed the steel, design, and so forth. It then improved its existing product. A few months later, the HAM purchaser was so impressed with the new product that he gave Honda's jack specs to the manufacturer. Today, this company has a contract to produce all of the jacks for the Civics and Accords made in Ohio. The company plans to export some of them to Japan soon.

Each spring, HAM has a Vendor's Appreciation Day. On May 6, 1987, more than two hundred suppliers and guests attended the event during which twenty-three awards were presented to eighteen companies. Awards were given in four different categories: quality, delivery, cost improvement, and special awards.

Inland Steel, for example, received a special award for its extensive efforts in developing a special type of steel for use at HAM; another went to WAK Plastics for great quality control efforts that resulted in a significant increase in the quality of its parts; and Stanley Electric was a recipient for its 100 percent record of on-time delivery for the three-year period 1984 to 1986. During the day, several vendors made NH Circle presentations.

FROM TINY ACORNS GROW
MIGHTY OAKS

In 1975, even before Ohio officials made their trip to Japan to scout for an automobile manufacturer, Capitol Plastics of Ohio, Inc., had contacted Honda. At the time, the small Bowling Green company's sales were about $5 million, a drop in the bucket for a manufacturer expecting to do business on an international scale.

Capitol president Bill Taylor explains: "We knew the Japanese were going to be here in the United States on a permanent basis, so we figured we should try to do business with them. Back then, we didn't know Honda had any plans to build a plant in Ohio, but we were impressed with the quality of its motorcycles. We thought someday it might have a factory somewhere in the United States. So even before the company opened its temporary offices in Columbus, we began sending letters to them."

Honda acknowledged Capitol's letters, but that was it; there was nothing to indicate even a trace of interest. About a year before construction of the Marysville plant began, Capitol received its first encouraging response. The small plastics firm was granted an appointment to meet with American Honda in California. In an effort to put its best foot forward, Capitol put together a brief audiovisual presentation. It also compiled some literature about its business. After the meeting, Capitol mailed more letters, but no orders came in. Then, after the Columbus offices were set up, Capitol representatives persistently made in-person calls. "We persevered," Taylor says with a smile. "I'm sure they accumulated the highest pile of correspondence from us on their desks, and frankly I think they thought the only way to get rid of all that paper was to give us a contract.

"But before an order was placed, a team of purchasing people visited us in Bowling Green to inspect and review everything. I estimate that 150 people must have come through here, including some Japanese directors from Honda Motor Company. While their requests seemed unusual to us, we turned over everything they wanted to examine. For instance, they asked to see a detailed cost breakdown of our proposals. In the past, other manufacturers only looked at the bottom line, not how we got there. As it turned out, Honda's managers compared our cost structure with ones they received from other companies, and they studied our efficiencies. With this information, they'd come back and make suggestion after suggestion on ways we could improve. Someone would say, for example, 'This is the way we manufacture it in Japan. Maybe you should consider this and then resubmit your proposal.'"

Taylor estimates that it was nearly three years after Capitol's first contact with Honda before the first order was placed. It was for a Fender B, a small, black fender that went under the back seat of the motorcycle. The first shipment carried an invoice for $238.

"If I were to put a dollar value on the human hours of engineering time, sales proposals, management meetings, and so on, we probably invested $200,000 to get that first order," Taylor tells. "It was like a poker game where you have to stay in for the next card. But from the beginning we were determined to do whatever it would take to do business with Honda."

According to Taylor, Capitol and Honda today have an unusual rapport that resembles a partnership more than a seller-customer relationship. Not surprisingly, Capitol's rapid growth has caused several problems, ranging from quality control to overexpansion. In each case, Honda teams were dispatched to Bowling Green to work side by side with Capitol employees to implement changes and exchange production philosophies.

"Honda is constantly observing our performance," Taylor expresses, "and as we improve, we're requested to submit more quotations to the company. It's a good system. As we grow, Honda increases its business with us. Naturally, we're expected to make improvements along the way. As the quality of our work improved, Honda placed more orders for different parts. At first we made nonvisible parts, but today we manufacture highly visible interior parts such as consoles and dash panels. We even make exterior parts, including the grill. Honda categorizes each of its suppliers—some only produce parts with no aesthetic significance."

Taylor points out that Honda has a strong loyalty to its suppliers, and a strong bond develops over a period of time. He states that today Capitol is considered a dedicated supplier, meaning that if the demand for Honda automobiles were to drop, less business would be awarded to smaller suppliers in favor of the larger ones. "It's a matter of Honda looking out for the vendors that depend on Honda's business versus another that does only a small amount of business with HAM. Honda is interested in building long-term relationships with those vendors that are committed, dedicated, and loyal. Like a partner, Honda's purchasing people work closely with us in developing our long-term projections. Consequently, we have a fairly good idea what is expected of us at least two years in advance."

As a result of HAM's enormous expansion program, Capitol also has prospered. Its production has increased sixfold. During its pre-Honda days it had only two injection molding machines; today there are twenty-six. The company originally made one part for Honda, but today produces more than eighty parts. The number of employees on the payroll has increased from about 120 to 350.

Today, an estimated 41 percent of Capitol's total production goes to Honda. The vendor's second largest customer is Chrysler, which accounts for about 30 percent. Other clients include General Motors and Toyota's joint venture NUMMI in Fremont, California, and Mazda's new plant in Flat Rock, Michigan. While some auto makers frown on its vendors doing business with competing companies out of fear of losing a competitive edge, or having confidential design information get into the wrong hands, Honda has no such objections.

"There is no doubt that our relationship with Honda has made us a far better company," Taylor says, "and as a consequence, Capitol is more appealing to other auto manufacturers. Due to our work with Honda, our increased volume of business has created a much greater base over which we can spread our costs, and the economies of scale of production have made us more profitable."

Since HAM's first order to Capitol in 1979, HAM has mushroomed from a relatively small motorcycle plant to America's fourth largest auto maker. Long-term plans call for continued growth, which also means larger orders for Capitol. Accordingly, Honda introduced Capitol managers to officials from Moriroku Company Ltd., a highly respected $600 million Japanese company and a major Honda plastics supplier. With HAM's increased production, Honda suggested that Moriroku and Capitol join forces and enter a technical collaboration agreement, a joint venture in which the two companies could operate a new American plant. After managers of both companies made several trips back and forth to get acquainted, Taylor said, "Each side liked what it saw and decided to follow Honda's advice."

Taylor, who has worked closely with Honda for several years, notes, "Everything its people do is well thought out with an eye on what effect it will have on long-term planning. Sometimes I feel as though I never really know what's in the back of their minds, but I do realize that they're thinking about something distant. Little by little, they begin to feed pieces of their long-term plan to us, and then when the entire program is revealed, I think to myself: 'By golly, they've been planning to do this all the time.' I truly admire how Honda managers always are thinking ahead."

The result of the collaboration is Greenville Technology, Inc., a new plastics molding plant in Ohio owned and operated by Moriroku and Capitol. It is located in Greenville, about 50 miles west of HAM. So far, all three parties, Capitol, Moriroku, and Honda, appear delighted with the new venture.

THE WORLD'S GREATEST ADVERTISING ACCOUNT

Perhaps more than any other field, the advertising industry is associated with ulcers. And deservingly so. Just observe the number of ad agencies that get the axe during a downswing in the economy, or when a certain company doesn't get its expected market share in a given period. Rather than admitting their own shortcomings, corporate managers frequently blame their ad agencies. Instead of admitting to a weak marketing program, poor service, or an inferior product, it's goodbye agency!

"Honda is different," insists Gerry Rubin, president of Rubin Postaer & Associates. "Their managers are interested in building long-term relationships, and they treat our agency with the same closeness as they would a partner. We receive the same tender care they extend to their customer. It is a special relationship that advertising people rarely experience. As a consequence, we don't have the constant fear that other agencies experience with their major accounts, and I believe the end result is a better quality in our work. When an ad person is constantly forced to work under the gun, his or her creativity is bound to suffer. That kind of pressure is unnecessary, and it makes people nervous about taking risks."

Rubin has worked on the Honda account since 1973, and has served as the head of the Needham Harper agency's Los Angeles office. In 1986, when Needham Harper became part of a three-agency megamerger, the firm terminated its agreement with Honda because a major auto maker was an account of one of the merging agencies. Rubin and his partner, creative director Larry Postaer, formed a new agency, Rubin Postaer and Associates. They wasted little time in making a presentation to Honda.

Koichi Amemiya, executive vice-president of Honda's automobile division, headed a group of executives who listened to the new agency's presentation. A few minutes after Rubin was into it, Amemiya asked, "Are the people the same?"

"Yes," Rubin answered.

"Then there's no problem. The reason we have always had good communications with you is because you have good people."

The meeting was adjourned and Rubin Postaer became Honda's agency.

It's this brand of trust and confidence Amemiya exhibited that makes Rubin proudly state, "Honda is the world's greatest advertising account."

13

Long-term Thinking

SINCE making its bold entry into the automobile industry, Honda has achieved meteoric success in an unprecedented period of time. In less than a quarter of a century, the company has emerged as one of the world's foremost auto makers. Achievement of this magnitude is the result of careful and methodical planning. Honda's sustained growth will continue, if management can set and secure its long-term objectives.

Honda's concern for its future can, in part, be traced to its Japanese roots. Of the phrase *mottainai* (to waste is a sin), Sony's chief executive officer, Akio Morita, says, "We Japanese feel that all things are provided as a sacred trust and actually are only loaned to us to make the best use of." He points out that Japan has almost no raw materials except water, and less than a quarter of the land is livable or arable. He also notes that Japan is 99.7 percent dependent on oil imports, 100 percent dependent for aluminum, iron ore, and nickel, more than 95 percent dependent for copper, and more than 92 percent dependent for natural gas. Morita says, "We Japanese are obsessed with survival."

It is no wonder that the Japanese plan their lives with an eye fixed on the future. This thinking is evident in all walks of life in Japan. For instance, the average Japanese puts about 20 percent of his or her disposable income each year into savings.

This figure is the highest rate of personal savings in any major nation, about four times as high as the average American saves.

The Japanese are among the most educated people in the world. Japan's illiteracy rate runs less than 2 percent, compared with about 20 percent in the United States. And Japan's best educated and most capable young people are likely to seek a position in government, in contrast to the United States, where more interest is in the private sector.

Today, Japanese industry and government continue to spend billions in energy R&D while Europe and America have discontinued energy projects in the face of falling oil prices. As an official from Japan's Natural Energy Resources Agency explains, "It shows how much of a crisis mentality Japan has over energy. We want to be prepared for the next oil crisis." Another Japanese official says, "Some are saying we should slow down, but the government's policy is that R&D has a long lead time and that we can't be swayed by the short-term energy situation."

High savings, emphasis on education, duty to country, investment in R&D—conviction to these doctrines reveals a people consumed with the future. Today's sacrifice and commitment determine tomorrow's destiny.

When considering the future is a matter of routine in making business decisions, it is bound to have a positive impact. This does not suggest that all Japanese business managers are driven by the constant thought that their company's survival is based on their present actions. To stereotype an entire nation is foolish. Nevertheless, culture does play a role in the daily transactions and conduct of a corporation. The management of the Honda Motor Company reflects certain attributes of its Japanese culture, among which is its perpetual concern with investing significant amounts of its present resources toward future endeavors.

The successful operation of an automobile company demands long-term planning. First, it is an immensely capital-intensive industry, so a manufacturer must commit large sums of money for machinery and equipment, many years before it realizes any return on its investment. Second, model designs are planned years before actual production. Third, sizable amounts of money are required for R&D in order to gain a technological edge over the competition. Like other auto makers, Honda's success hinges on its ability to plan years in advance of a new model's debut.

SHORT-TERM PROFITS VERSUS LONG-TERM GAINS

Publicly owned domestic corporations are frequently afflicted with "quarteritis," an often terminal disease in the business world. It is unfortunate, but somewhere along the way American business leaders began keeping score of their corporations' progress on a three-month basis. It's not only the shareholders that American companies must worry about—they've got to be concerned with what the Wall Street analysts and corporate raiders are thinking.

This is not the case in Japan. Japanese companies can afford to wait because they have allies in their big shareholders. These mainly are banks, insurance companies, and institutional investors who don't meddle in management and who don't press for short-term profitability or cost-cutting measures. The companies have the luxury of pumping money into research even if it hurts the balance sheets. Unlike stockholders, bankers do not stand to gain directly from a quick boost in corporate earnings or share prices; their main concern is that a company that has borrowed from them stays in business and continues to pay the interest on its debts.

When Kawasaki Steel Corporation posted a $330 million loss for its fiscal year ending March 31, 1987, managers' salaries were cut, mills were closed, and the capital investment was slashed. But the steel company's R&D wasn't touched. "Without research muscle, we have no future," says a Kawasaki research director. "We can't expect to start making profits in new businesses in just a few years." This strategy illustrates one of the strengths of the Japanese economy. Western manufacturers, especially in older industries, often cut costs across the board when profits fall. In Japan, where stockholders are patient, loans come easy and takeovers are rare. R&D in times of hardship is a must.

In similar straits, many big U.S. steel makers reduced R&D budgets. Bethlehem Steel Corporation cut its research in 1982 when it began to incur losses, and followed with further cuts in 1983 and 1984. The company sold its research center, reduced the number of researchers to 450 from nearly 1,000 in the 1960s, and moved many of the remaining employees out of central research laboratories and into the plants.

Although Japan's steel industry is experiencing hard times, another Japanese steel executive stresses, "We have to bite the bullet today to be able to eat tomorrow." He adds, "Steel will never grow like it did. If we don't open new areas, we can't survive."

It's not just Japan's smokestack industries that maintain R&D. The same attitude is expressed by executives in other fields. For example, a Japanese high-tech executive says: "If we don't do our R&D now, our sales in five years will be halved. It's like food—it's the last thing you cut out."

"When things get tough, the trend here is to focus even more on research," says a Japanese electronics executive. "Right now that's one of our weapons against the high yen."

Contrast this thinking to Chrysler's reduction of its R&D expenditures in 1987. Today, out of an estimated 100,000 employees, only 5,000 are in R&D. This figure compares to more than 8,000 employees who work in R&D at Honda, which has less than 60,000 employees in its worldwide work force. In fact, R&D at Honda consumes 5 percent of its annual earnings versus the automotive industry average of 3.5 percent, which is itself considerably higher than the U.S. average of less than 1.5 percent for all industries.

Takeomi Miyoshi, executive chief engineer at Honda's Tochigi R&D Center in Japan, says: "Our R&D operates as a separate entity that allows for creative freedom. We are isolated from outside voices (other Honda operations). R&D is a long-term operation."

Perhaps the Marysville plant itself is the best testimony of

Honda's long-term commitment to the United States and its own future. It was only three months after HAM's motorcycle production began in September 1979 that Honda Motor president, Kiyoshi Kawashima, in Tokyo proposed: "Now is the time that we should begin to plan to manufacture automobiles at the Marysville site." In January 1980, he publicly announced Honda's ambitious plans.

To reach this goal, Honda committed huge sums of money and many of its most able people. When HAM first began manufacturing automobiles in 1982, its daily production was ten cars a day. A decision had been made that rather than striving for mass production, the emphasis would be on quality workmanship. Even with its huge investment in its Ohio operation, Honda refused to give in to the temptation to increase production too rapidly. With its immense overhead at HAM, it was inevitable that the company would suffer sizable short-term losses. It simply wasn't economical to have a plant costing hundreds of millions of dollars that made a mere ten cars a day! Still, management refused to produce more cars until it was certain the quality was on par with those Honda models made in Japan.

Some people have suggested that Honda's motivation for manufacturing in the United States has been the strong yen. This is without merit, especially when one considers that the plant's original planning occurred back in the mid-1970s. As one auto industry observer explains, "You don't shift manufacturing bases around the world simply because of a short-term movement in the exchange rates."

While profit certainly is not a dirty word among the members of Honda's upper management, the philosophy of focusing on long-term gains instead of short-term profits is one that has permeated all facets of of daily operations. Each new associate is recruited with a view to the future. The sizable expenses incurred to send new trainees to Honda plants in Japan demonstrates the company's willingness to invest large sums of money in people *before* those people have earned their stripes. This up-front approach again is witnessed in the servicing of customers at the dealer level. Sales and repair people are trained to win customers by viewing each car buyer as a lifetime customer rather than as a single sale. Long-term thinking is the core of how business is conducted throughout the Honda world. It's not a fancy advertising slogan or a snow job by an aggressive public relations department. It is a way of life.

In an interview in *Barron's Weekly* in late 1985, Honda North America President Tetsuo Chino discussed what he termed his corporate goal:

> ... to establish Honda in America as an American corporation. Americanization of production is part of that, of course. But we also do R&D here to make sure our cars are accepted by the American people. We also want to Americanize our capital, which means we are going to reinvest a good portion of our profit in this country. And last but not least, we want to Americanize management. Ultimately, I would like to see Honda accepted as an American company.

Part of this "Americanization" has been realized. The domestic content of 1988 models produced at HAM is 60 percent and expected to increase to 75 percent by 1991. The present number of R&D people employed in the United States is 180 and is expected to increase to 500 by 1991. Honda recently spent $31 million to purchase the Transportation Research Center from the state of Ohio as a site for its second auto plant and as a focus for activities that will enable Honda to become a self-reliant motor vehicle manufacturer in the United States. The company has reinvested its profits in the United States—its total investment in Ohio is approaching the $2 billion mark. And today, the majority of managers are U.S.-born citizens.

A PHILOSOPHY OF SELF-SUFFICIENCY

Unlike most corporations, Honda has avoided the temptation to buy fundamental technology from outside sources. As Honda Motor Company president Kume points out, "It would appear cheaper to buy it, but when you do, the technology remains frozen, a foreign thing that is not part of yourself. In the end you don't know where to go with it." He explains that when a company has not developed the basics, it is forever relying on others, and in the long run the company does not control its own destiny.

Honda R&D executive chief engineer Miyoshi says, "While some of our Japanese competitors have incorporated what they have learned from companies abroad, they eventually put themselves in a vulnerable position where they can't expand their technology in certain areas because they lack the fundamentals."

This independence is best illustrated by the many technological innovations Honda has produced since first starting in business. Soichiro Honda, himself, produced more than 470 patented ideas and designs during his career.

Honda's automatic transmission design is a good example of how the company chooses to develop its own technology. Instead of entering licensing agreements for patents and technology, Honda engineers started from scratch. They came up with a lighter-weight, fuel-efficient, reliable transmission that is uniquely Honda's. And in more recent years, Honda Motor Company has had many engineering firsts in the areas of internal combustion systems, antilock braking systems, four-wheel steering systems, automatic transmissions, and aluminum die casting. Even the machinery that the company uses to manufacture its product is produced primarily by its wholly owned subsidiary, Honda Engineering.

Honda's chief executive officers have always been engineers. Kume says, "It is not that we ever decided to have a president with an engineering background, but an underlying concept of this firm is that rather than being driven to realize profits, we want to make superior engines. When a company thinks in these terms, its customers will be satisfied, and the profits eventually will be there too."

HAM president Irimajiri sums up Honda's constant drive to remain independent by saying, "We never will ask others to support us. We know how to motivate ourselves to perform one hundred percent, or more than one hundred percent, because we know we can decide our own destiny. We always will carry our own torch."

SETTING, REVIEWING, ADJUSTING, AND COMMUNICATING GOALS

No long-term goal at Honda is ever cast in stone. Along the way, long-term plans are continually being reviewed and adjusted.

Irimajiri explains, "When we decide on a production schedule, we always set a long-term target to shoot for. We then set up checkpoints along the way, and if the trend indicates that we will achieve our goal, we continue to go full steam toward that objective.

"For example, when an annual budget or some other short-term program is reviewed, the company's top management frequently will meet with our lower-level people who become the actual implementers. Questions are asked such as: 'What is the present progress?' 'What is the trend of the program?' 'Is it on target to meet our ultimate objective?' 'What do you anticipate will be the final result?' The answers to these questions determine if a project or production schedule will be permitted to continue as originally planned."

After Honda's top management establishes a long-term goal, many lower level people are brought in to participate in implementing it. In the manufacturing end of the business, for example, senior management informs department managers and coordinators about company goals and its long-range plans. Department managers and coordinators then are requested to contribute their ideas and this information comes back up to senior management for review. Soon everyone has an awareness of the long-term goals and what is needed to accomplish them.

14

Nothing Is Constant but Change

IT is a contradiction to say that change is constant. But to Honda, it is a mere paradox.

When the Honda Motor Company Ltd. was founded in 1948, it bought and rebuilt small, used gasoline engines to attach to bicycles. The following year, the company manufactured its own 50-cc, two-cycle engines, and in 1951, it introduced a breakthrough design with a new version of the four-stroke engine. The next year, Honda began producing motorcycle frames, chains, and sprockets. By the end of the decade, Honda had emerged as the world's largest motorcycle company. Then, in 1960, the company entered the automobile industry. Honda's is a story of constant change.

Once it is accepted as inevitable, change should be eagerly anticipated, never resisted. With this kind of attitude, people can accept it as a condition of their employment; it comes with the territory.

Professionals in every field understand the need to anticipate. Wayne Gretzky, who is considered the greatest hockey player in the sport's history, once was asked his secret of success. He replied, "I skate to where the puck is going to be, not where it has been."

Honda's management is geared to respond quickly. Many

years ago when the company chose never to depend on outside sources for its fundamental technology, a commitment was made to be a leader in the automotive field. To its management, there was no alternative. To react to change after the fact is following, not leading. This belief explains the company's willingness to spend such a high percentage of its annual gross revenue on R&D.

As the Red Queen said in Lewis Carroll's *Alice Through the Looking Glass:* "Now, here you see, it takes all the running you can do to keep in the same place. If you want to get somewhere else, you must run twice as fast." This advice is well followed at Honda where people fully understand that standing still is going backward.

The Honda of yesteryear was a different company than it is today. And the Honda of the future is certain to be a different company than the one that exists now. The company's zeal for change, a constant effort to stay ahead of its competition, can be compared to a race car driver who is six laps ahead of the field, but keeps racing as if he or she is behind by six laps. In this respect, a "paranoia" exists within the Honda organization. Perhaps the attitude is a legacy passed down by the company's founder who demanded the constant development of new technology to keep his company from perishing. In a nineteenth-century poem, "The *Mary Gloster*," Rudyard Kipling wrote: "They copied all they could follow / But they couldn't copy my mind / And I left 'em sweating and stealing / A year and a half behind." Such is the heritage of Honda.

THE IMPORTANCE OF SPEED

HAM president Shoichiro Irimajiri is fond of using auto racing analogies when talking about Honda. He credits the company's racing success to adjusting to change. Irimajiri states, "Rules in both business and racing are always being changed. There have been many instances when, after a Honda victory, our competition has changed the rules to benefit it in a future race. For example, after our six-cylinder engines became top winners in motorcycle racing, other manufacturers banded together to limit Grand Prix entries to four-cylinder engines. Then, when we won the 50-cc motorcycle Grand Prix with the 12-speed transmission, again they banded together and reduced it to a 6-speed transmission.

"Later, when we won the Formula Two auto racing with a 2-liter engine, they changed the rules to require a 3-liter engine. The same thing is happening with Honda's dominance of the Formula One racing with our twin turbo-charged engines. It's now been changed to nonturbo-charged engines, and the engine's capacity is 3.5 liters instead of 1.5 liters. So in the world of racing, when one company rises above the crowd, the rules are liable to be changed.

"The rules keep changing in the world of business, too, frequently in areas where we have little or no control. For instance, the yen-dollar exchange rate keeps fluctuating. And various governments keep revising the tariff rules."

Honda Motor Company president Tadashi Kume says the company doesn't try to dispute any changes that occur in the racing circuit. "That's fine. We will make whatever adjustments are necessary and we will win again." The CEO feels that rule changes in racing serve as a challenge, and thus are good preparation for the business world.

Soichiro Honda understood this: "On one side, we have the customer who is always changing," he'd stress. "And on the other side, technology is changing. To survive in the automobile industry, we must change before our competitors. It is the auto maker who makes the fastest changes that wins."

Irimajiri emphasizes that as the world becomes more crowded, its marketplace becomes more competitive, and the fastest-moving manufacturers and managers are the ones most likely to survive. He points out that in only a short span of ten years, the American automobile market increased from mainly domestic competition to what it is today. "Look how drastically things have changed," Irimajiri claims. "There are many automobile manufacturers selling cars in America today. There are the European companies with such cars as the Mercedes, BMW, Audi, plus many Japanese companies. Now cars from Korea, Yugoslavia, Malaysia, Taiwan, and other countries are entering the U.S. market, and there are rumors that even the Soviet Union will sell their cars here in the not-too-distant future. The competition is getting more abundant and more fierce all the time. The winners will be those companies that respond quickly to change."

Time after time, Honda has demonstrated its ability to respond with lightening speed. Take, for instance, the company's all-out effort to develop the CVCC engine when the Clean Air Act was about to become the law of the land in the United States. Within a single year, Honda's eight-man team met the Act's requirements with an engine that did not require a catalytic converter, and in the process, gained a technological lead in the automotive market place that it has never lost.

Then, in early 1984, Honda announced its decision to more than double the capacity of HAM. The company could not afford to shut the plant down, and to make matters even more challenging, the completion of the expanded plant was coordinated with a major model change in the Accord scheduled for September 1985.

On September 19, 1985, HAM made automotive history in the United States. At the same time the last 1985 Accord was being driven off the assembly line, the first 1986 Accord—a completely new model—was starting down the assembly line. It was a mind-boggling achievement. Not only had the auto company made a major model change in a single night, but this was accomplished with the distraction of construction work.

ACCEPTING CHANGE AS THE NORM

People in the marketing end of the automobile business anticipate change. But this is not common at the typical manufacturing site. At HAM, however, associates must readily accept change. HAM's vice-president, Al Kinzer, explains, "In 1979, all of the jobs were different than they are today. Because of the ongoing advances in automation and the production line changes, associates must be flexible because their present jobs are going to be different tomorrow." There are scores of stories of HAM associates who originally worked in the motorcycle department and who later were transferred to the automobile assembly line. And today many of these same men and women can be found working at the engine plant at Anna, Ohio.

Of course, change is an annual occurrence when new procedures are introduced for Honda's new line of models. One associate says, "Each year, just when I feel things have leveled off after having made our production goal, everything has to be changed for the new model. It always amazes me to see the technology changed to increase quality and efficiency."

An avid golfer, Irimajiri compares the steady influx of change to a round of golf. "Here is the tee and over here is the green. The hole on the green is the ultimate goal, but exactly how you reach it depends on many factors. Your drive and your iron shots naturally will influence what happens between your tee shot and how you play the hole. You also may come across an obstacle such as a sand trap or a pond. In the plant, we also know exactly where we want to go, but we must remain flexible and make changes along the way to get there."

Change is accepted as the norm at Honda. Plant associates are told that they should never accept what is being done simply because it has been done that way in the past. They should always try to make improvements. This philosophy applies to everyone who works at Honda.

Indeed, Honda's enormous commitment to do business in the United States illustrates its adaptability to change. Many changes are mandatory in order to succeed as a major manufacturer and marketer of automobiles in this country. Vast differences in both social mores and business practices face those Honda managers who are transplanted to the United States. For example, the use of legal services varies greatly between the two countries, in particular in attitudes toward litigation. As Shelley Lanza, general counsel at HAM, points out: "In Japan many business deals are made with a handshake rather than a long, written document. At first, our Japanese managers had difficulty understanding a lawyer's role in the negotiations with vendors and why lengthy contracts were necessary."

The contrast is made clear when observing that there are approximately 600,000 attorneys in the United States, and each year another estimated 40,000 people pass the bar examinations. In Japan, there are approximately 17,000 lawyers with only about 300 persons annually passing the bar examination. (Note that less than 3 percent pass in Japan.) And keep in mind that the U.S. population is roughly twice Japan's. While the United States has been busy creating lawyers, Japan has been busier creating engineers. Annually, there are twice as many engineering graduates in Japan as in the United States.

Vendors who build long-term relationships with Honda are similarly attuned to accept change. The parts supplier that is most likely to succeed in its dealings with Honda is one that immediately begins to find ways to improve quality and lower or maintain costs. In turn, the improvements and savings are passed on to Honda. This is in strong contrast to the many American companies that rarely offer improvements once the dotted line is signed. And it represents a striking difference from those companies that expect cost-of-living price increases to be built in automatically.

THE EVER-EXPANDING AUTO PLANT

Perhaps no Honda changes are more visible than the constant construction of the HAM plant itself. Since the ground-breaking of the 260,000-square-foot motorcycle plant in 1978, construction crews have been seen on the site every single working day. Shortly after the motorcycle plant was built, construction was underway to build a one-million-square-foot, $250 million auto plant. In 1982, after the first Accord rolled off the assembly line, plans were being drawn to add another 1 million square feet for a second line of HAM-made Civics that began production in 1986. And, as of this writing, a $380 million plant is being constructed for a third production line that is estimated to begin producing cars in August 1989.

Jack Ruscilli, CEO of Ruscilli Construction, the Columbus-based firm that built a 1.4-million-square-foot addition to HAM's original auto plant, says, "It was a unique job because everything had to be coordinated with Honda's people in Japan to accommodate the installation of the automobile manufacturing equipment. It was essential to have precision timing of the construction and the delivery of machinery, and this was accomplished with some very sophisticated computerized control systems. Otherwise, it would have been impossible for us to stay on top of everything."

"It's no easy matter to construct a huge building around an automobile manufacturing line that's operating at full production," concurs Ruscilli's president, E. J. Edminister. "With one car coming through the construction area every 58 seconds, we had to be very careful to avoid spraying one of them with concrete or anything like that. The construction workers had a joke: 'Spray it and you own it.' "

According to Ruscilli, communications was a constant problem during the construction that lasted from April 1984 to April 1986. "There were probably as many as fifty different Honda engineers from Japan who were assigned to the project," he says. "It was a horrendous job to extract information from these individuals who basically spoke little English, and quite often, the translation was watered down through interpreters. To make matters more confusing, after working with certain engineers for a few months when we were just beginning to communicate adequately, they were sent back to Tokyo and replaced by new engineers.

"I recall one meeting when it took forty-five minutes to communicate the difference between an overhead door and a shutter. They thought we were talking about a shutter while all the time we were discussing an overhead door, and consequently, everyone was totally confused."

The most difficult part of constructing the enormous addition, however, was dealing with the changes that were constantly occurring. "The demand for Honda cars was so great" explains Ruscilli, "that the plans for our addition kept changing to accommodate anticipated higher production. For instance, at one meeting while we were reviewing our plot plant, to our surprise, we were told, 'No, that's where our new plastics plant will be.'

" 'No, it isn't,' I replied. 'The recently completed test track is there.'

" 'Not now,' a Honda engineer replied, 'The plastics plant goes there now.'

"So we had to shift gears and put in a $40 million plastics plant in that spot and relocate the test track. The track was moved three times during the course of the job."

Throughout the construction, Honda's engineers continually updated specifications to meet the needs of new production equipment being developed in Japan. "They were always designing and coming up with something better," Ruscilli says. "Yet, despite the changes, each original deadline had to be met. Honda's people never wanted to hear about moving a date back."

The result was that every construction deadline was met.

Working with Honda taught Ruscilli a good lesson about flexibility and being able to respond to change. "There's an attitude at Honda that dictates, 'Everything is possible,' " Ruscilli tells. "Well, we did the impossible, and it's changed our entire thinking. Due to our experience with Honda, we're a much better company today."

COMMUNICATING CHANGE

In general, people resist change because they feel comfortable with the old and familiar way, and because they don't want to risk accepting something that might not be as good as the existing way. Uncertainty causes doubt and confusion, so it's much easier to maintain the status quo. Resistance is likely to accompany any change, unless management properly communicates change.

In every large organization, people must be kept abreast from within. At Honda, constant communication lets associates know that change is a natural, everyday occurrence, and everyone participates in it. Indeed, physical change is highly visible at HAM. Since its original groundbreaking in 1979, not a single day has passed without the presence of construction people on the site—a perpetual reminder that change is constant.

Honda adheres to the principle that people will support what they helped to create. By getting associates involved in the early stages of projects, Honda smoothes the transition to the new. When a company's employees learn from outside sources about major changes in their employer's future, and subsequently their futures as well, they often feel insecure and feel they have no control over their own future.

Change at Honda is gradual and steady and not something that descends on its people in one massive swoop. Susan Insley, HAM's vice-president of corporate planning, explains: "Since the first days when HAM was producing ten cars a day, communications have focused on how production would increase, and as a result our associates are able to comfortably adjust to the new production goals. If they were simply told that the production was being upped by some staggering amount, say 200,000 units for the year, the number could overwhelm them. We are not going to go from here to there in a single day. In fact, we have days when we will not go forward, but instead go backward a little, but over a period of time we keep going steadily forward step by step. Everyone in the plant understands change and knows why we are doing it."

HAM's executive vice-president, Toshi Amino, believes that Honda attracts a certain type of worker who thrives on change. "There's a hunger for change here," he explains, "and we've become conditioned to the challenge it creates. So many people here need this kind of excitment—it's a part of the Honda culture."

AN OBSESSION WITH BIGNESS

"Big, not best, has always been the American calling card," Tom Peters writes in *Thriving on Chaos.* "I bet you can't drive more than seventy-five miles in any direction, from anywhere in the United States, without running into a 'biggest in the world' of some sort." He goes on to say that this all-American system, with long production runs and mass operations, paid off with victories in World Wars I and II, and cemented subsequent U.S. economic dominance. After all, wars were won with *more* tanks and planes, not *better* ones.

Listen to the chatter when the Fortune 500 comes out. Few chiefs comment on their profits or returns on assets. The question is: "What's your rank?" Making the Fortune 500, an achievement based on size alone, is the Holy Grail for most nonmembers; moving up is the Holy Grail for most members.

In the United States, change and progress are too often measured by sheer size, not quality. Fast food restaurants and retail stores keep score by how many outlets they open each year. The nation's major law firms and accounting firms measure their successes by their total number of partners and associates. Some book publishers rank themselves according to the number of books published each year.

But the world has changed in the past four decades, and today the emphasis must be placed on quality, not just quantity. If the United States is to remain a dominant economic power, corporate America must measure change in terms of how quality improves each year. Restaurants and retail stores should think more in terms of service. Attorneys, accountants, publishers, and all working Americans must readjust their thinking and concentrate on what Peters describes as the bottom line:

> If you can't point to something specific that's being done differently from the way it was done when you came to work this morning, you have not "lived," for all intents and purposes; you surely have not earned your paycheck by any stretch of the imagination.

Takeo Fujisawa, Honda's cofounder, repeatedly said his dream was the creation of an organization that always would maintain the spirit and vitality of a small company. Soichiro Honda shared this dream. Neither man had the goal of building a big corporation, nor were they driven by ambitions to generate huge profits. Both, however, welcomed change, and understood that the company's survival was dependent on how it would be accepted by people in an ever-changing world.

THINKING GLOBALLY IN A CHANGING WORLD

In 1954, when the Honda Motor Company was only six years old, its founder declared that it would be an international company. This has guided its management to think globally in the making of all long-term decisions. Cedrick Shimo, vice-president of Honda International Trading, Inc., explains, "Our survival depends on global thinking. Our late entry into the automobile industry made it difficult for us to compete against the already established automobile manufacturers in Japan. We had no choice but to look at the entire world as our marketplace, and it was this thinking that motivated us to establish a manufacturing plant in the United States."

Today, Honda sells its products all over the world. The company's competition also is worldwide. "Our products are made to compete in world markets," Irimajiri explains. "Thus it is events in the world which shape our market and our products, not just events in our city, state, or country."

In the late 1960s, shortly after the company began manufacturing automobiles, Soichiro Honda announced that he wanted to make a world car. To accomplish this, the company sent two teams of engineers to travel around the world to collect data about products and life-styles of people in other countries. In conjunction with this program, Honda's R&D sent engineers to Europe with instructions to spend a full year there doing nothing but observing the relationship between the citizens of those countries and their automobiles. The engineers studied everything from road conditions to driving habits. Then they returned to Japan to report their findings. This information helped Honda to design the first Civic, which it appropriately referred to as a "world car."

Later, in the mid-1970s, in preparation for the introduction of the first Accords in the United States, Honda engineers were dispatched to the Los Angeles area to study American freeways. These engineers gathered pieces of asphalt from the Santa Monica freeway, measured dimensions of the road and the exit ramps, then returned to the company's testing grounds in Japan. There they built a replica of a few miles of the Santa Monica freeway that was so exact that minute details such as expansion joints and road signs were included. This research made it possible for Honda to conduct road tests on the Accord's performance under the same freeway conditions it would experience in Southern California, these conditions being vastly different than Japan's.

Honda's global thinking offers a timely message for corporate managers in today's America. Survival may rest on how they adopt new views of the changing world marketplace. Limited thinking that confines marketing within the borders of the United States no longer works. Companies that fail to think globally are doomed to go the way of the dinosaur.

American industry is losing ground to foreign companies at an alarming rate. A continued trade imbalance is bound to have serious repercussions. Some have proposed imposing tariffs on imports, raising taxes, and reducing government spending. While these actions may provide some immediate benefits, they are only temporary remedies. Long-term solutions will not come through government legislation, but rather through corporate America's capacity to compete favorably in a world marketplace. In this respect, Honda, with an eye on the future, is an ideal model for U.S. companies.

There is much to be learned about the world marketplace. In the same way that Honda carefully studied our culture and life-style, so must American corporate managers do their homework. For starters, it is helpful to speak the language in those countries where they plan to market their products. American companies also can become more familiar with various cultures around the world by establishing programs that send large numbers of students abroad. For example, barely 800 U.S. citizens are studying at Japanese universities. Yet according to the National Science Foundation, there are some 13,000 Japanese attending U.S. universities. Of course, a program that dispatches large numbers of students to the far ends of the world is certain to take years to bring results and it also will be quite costly. But many short-term sacrifices are necessary to achieve certain long-term results. We must learn to invest in our future.

The most important way to increase competitiveness is through the quality of products and services. In a truly competitive world marketplace, survival rightfully will belong to those companies that fulfill the needs of the customer. The associates working at HAM prove the American workers' capacity to compete head-on with the best workmanship and productivity of any work force in the world. If other companies endeavor to have a sequel to HAM's success, the overhauling of some leadership and attitudes is long overdue.

Fortunately, America has received the warning signals. What must be done is clear, and there still is time to respond. If we fail to act now, we must resign ourselves to becoming a second-rate economic power.

IV

A Corporate Philosophy

15

The Honda Way

OR THIS BOOK, nearly two hundred Honda associates in the United States and Japan were asked to comment on the Honda Way.

This request prompted a multiplicity of reactions. Some spoke casually, others with reverence. No matter what the response, the Honda Way touched everyone—those on the plant floor, at the R&D center, in the marketing offices, everywhere. Yet interpretations differ, even those of senior managers at the company's highest levels. An executive vice-president referred to it as a spirit; another top-ranking officer called it a dream; and yet another described it as a feeling. One senior manager said the Honda Way is impossible to describe: "It could be expressed only through Honda products."

What can be said about the Honda Way is that it distinguishes the Honda Motor Company from other corporations in Japan, the United States, or any other country. In part, it is the philosophy originated by Soichiro Honda and Takeo Fujisawa that has permeated the organization. And it is a corporate culture that over the years has evolved and endured. Based on definite values and beliefs, the Honda Way not only provides a strong company identity but it guides behavior.

The Honda Way influences every significant decision made throughout the entire organization. As both internal and external changes occur, these principles and beliefs provide associates with a common and consistent sense of direction. The Honda Way has far more to do with the company's success than any technological or economic resources. The Honda Way comprises many different beliefs, none of which is unique. Rather, it is the application of these beliefs that is uniquely Honda.

In his book, *The IBM Way,* Buck Rodgers, the former vice-president of IBM marketing, says a business must develop a set of principles on which to build before it can become a success. Rodgers quotes Tom Watson, Jr., the company founder's son and successor, as saying, "For any organization to survive and achieve success, there must be a sound set of principles on which it bases all of its policies and actions. But more important is its faithful adherence to those principles."

Rodgers says that an organization's only sacred cow should be its principles, which must remain unaltered. No matter what the company's nature or size, certain bedrock beliefs must serve as the guiding force. While a business must be flexible, always regrouping and changing with the times, its beliefs remain irrevocable, deeply embedded throughout time.

Everything else, of course, is subject to change. Companies change management, names, and locations. Product lines are subject to change. IBM, for example, originally manufactured butcher scales and time clocks. DuPont Chemical was America's largest supplier of gunpowder from the War of 1812 until the end of World War I. Rockwell International, a large aerospace company, first manufactured parking and taxi meters. And American Express began as a pony express. But a stable philosophy ultimately will determine an organization's greatness.

Rarely does a company's founder write down a corporate philosophy for future generations. In the beginning, there are more urgent and pressing matters, such as generating enough revenues to pay current bills. In 1948, Soichiro Honda was much too busy searching for used engines to think about what later would be known as the Honda Way. And the auto mechanic did not have the formal education or the business acumen to recognize the need for a corporate philosophy.

Corporate beliefs often are expressed in simple slogans such as the following:

G.E.: "Progress Is Our Most Important Product."
DuPont: "Better Things for Better Living Through Chemistry."
Sears, Roebuck: "Quality at a Good Price."
Dana Corporation: "Productivity Through People."

The Honda Way is neither a formalized, written set of beliefs nor a philosophy stated in a clever slogan or platitude. It is a collection of principles and ideals that have permeated the organization around the world.

For the remainder of this book, the Honda Way is explained in the most explicit portrayal ever disclosed to outsiders or ever published within the company. Yet this chapter does not necessarily represent *the* official presentation. It would be presumptuous to attempt such a writing because the Honda Way is truly both spirit and dream.

AN INTERNATIONAL VIEWPOINT

In 1954, when Honda was only six years old, it adopted an international viewpoint dedicating itself to supplying highly efficient products at reasonable prices worldwide. Honda products are made to compete in world markets that demand the finest quality.

This international approach often is referred to as the cornerstone of Honda's corporate philosophy. This viewpoint is what prompted Honda to build HAM in spite of a financial analysis that prognosticated the company could not make a profit manufacturing in the United States. When asked why he made the decision, President Kawashima said, "Because it was consistent with our corporate philosophy of manufacturing in the market we serve." As a part of this philosophy, the company believes that those who buy Honda products should have the opportunity to build Honda products.

This international philosophy also means making a commitment to the community. (In a broad sense, America is the community.) This is demonstrated by Honda's $2 billion investment in the United States, and through its plans to increase the domestic content of automobiles manufactured in the United States to 75 percent by 1991.

RESPECT FOR THE INDIVIDUAL

Honda's egalitarian environment, as described in chapter 6, is no accident. There are no us-them adversarial relationships between the management and work force. Everyone is treated as an equal, regardless of rank or position.

People involvement plays a crucial part in the philosophy. Honda's racing activities have greatly influenced the idea of teamwork in the plant itself. Just as the drivers, mechanics, and engineers must work together with clockwork precision to win the race, so must all employees join ranks to build and sell excellent automobiles.

This philosophy also is demonstrated by a respect for each individual's intelligence, hard work, and commitment. Production associates are considered the key to Honda's manufacturing success.

Effective management is based on trust. Everyone shares a sense of pursuing a common goal, and each individual has a specific role that contributes to that goal. For this reason, the company invites its people to participate during both the planning and the implementing of long-term goals. These goals are constantly communicated to associates throughout the organization.

A supervisor can show respect for his or her associates by allowing them to make mistakes. When an associate errs, the supervisor then asks, "What did I do wrong?"

Giving responsibility to people is perhaps the supreme vote of confidence in them. It makes people feel good about themselves, and when they do, they feel good about the company.

FACING THE TOUGHEST CHALLENGES
FIRST

Had Soichiro Honda shied away from tough challenges, there never would have been a Honda Motor Company. In 1948, the tiny motorcycle firm, with its small capitalization, faced insurmountable odds in an overcrowded Japanese marketplace with 247 other companies.

This philosophy demands first tackling those challenges deemed to be the most difficult. Honda's philosophy later was carried over to the marketing side of the business when in 1959 the company accepted the challenge to enter the world's largest market: the United States. A short time later, the company made the bold decision to sell automobiles in the world's most competitive and mature industry.

Later, Honda dared to manufacture motorcycles and automobiles on American soil. Honda also was the first foreign company to manufacture automobile engines in the United States, and the first to build a second automobile plant in the United States.

Risk taking is not only encouraged at Honda but associates are repeatedly told that failure should never be feared. "Only through failure can precious experience be gained," Soichiro Honda advocated. "But be sure to always learn from your mistakes." In an acceptance speech for a special award from the Japanese Ministry of Science for developing the CVCC, Honda said, "Failure by itself is not necessarily failure. We learn that we failed because we took a certain route, and this is how we now know what route we then must take to succeed."

FOSTERING AN ENTREPRENEURIAL
SPIRIT

As the company grows, everyone at Honda is reminded that new challenges always must be accepted and failure must never be feared. The tradition of the company's past achievements is perpetuated by the constant praising of trailblazers.

While Honda today is a multinational corporation, the company must continue to maintain those same characteristics it displayed as a small enterprise. "We have grown by using simple, straightforward production techniques," associates are told, "and we must never forsake these commendable entrepreneurial qualities."

To sustain a vital organization, the company has resisted tight home office controls over its faraway plants and divisions. Instead, management is decentralized, and responsibilities are delegated to those in charge of day-to-day operations. Each division has the freedom to be aggressive and innovative, and, accordingly, each contributes to the company's overall success. Problems are solved by the people at each plant, with small groups and divisions operating as small, independent businesses.

ON-THE-SPOT MANAGEMENT

A popular Honda saying is: "There is more knowledge on the plant floor than in the office." Managers understand that problems in the factory rarely are solved behind a desk or in a conference room. "Go to where the action is," they are advised. Managers go to the plant's trouble spot to see the problem firsthand. There, they actually can touch the malfunctioning part and speak with the associates involved. Only then can managers effectively contribute to solving problems.

HAM associates who have management responsibilities spend most of their day on the plant floor, where the plant's engineers also work almost exclusively. No manager hides behind closed doors in a far-removed executive suite. Even the factory's president spends a major portion of his or her time on the plant floor. A high level of responsibility is given to managers at all company subsidiaries because it is those managers who are on the spot.

This style of management isn't drawn from a textbook. It has been practiced by both Honda and Fujisawa since the company's early days. Honda came by it honestly through his humble beginnings as a worker in his father's blacksmith shop and as the owner of a tiny repair shop. He never hesitated to get his hands dirty with the grease of oily machines and engines. He spent the majority of his career working side by side with associates on the plant floor. And he was there in the pits during the company's early racing days; later he could be found supervising the tear-down of a racing engine. How well he understood the gap that existed between theory and reality: "You see what's real when you're on the spot," he preached.

And Fujisawa, executive vice-president in charge of finances and business for twenty-four years, rarely was behind his desk. He, too, spent a high percentage of his time reviewing new products at the R&D center. This on-the-spot management style is evident today in the company's marketing department, with executives regularly visiting dealers and customers.

ACCENT ON YOUTH

Honda is the largest company in Japan to have been founded since World War II, so by Japanese standards it is considered a young organization. Compared to the zaibatsu, which are huge, interconnected industrial complexes that have dominated the country's economy for centuries, Honda still is in its infancy. Entering the automobile field so late has prompted the company to always strive to be special in order to gain public acceptance.

Since its beginning, Honda has placed a strong accent on youth. The emphasis is on youthful thinking, and not necessarily on young people, though the average Honda manager is several years younger than the managers of other major automobile manufacturers.

During the 1950s, when Honda's success in the motorcycle industry necessitated the hiring of additional management, the company was unable to attract large numbers of experienced managers. It wasn't socially acceptable in Japan to work for a small business. At the time, a career with the up-and-coming maverick motorcycle company simply did not have the same prestige as a career with a zaibatsu organization. As a consequence, Honda promoted young people more quickly than other Japanese corporations did. The success of these young people prompted the company to delegate more authority to still more young associates. It has been this way ever since.

Takeo Fujisawa and Soichiro Honda officially retired in 1973 following the company's twenty-fifth anniversary, at age sixty-two and age sixty-six respectively. It was considered unusual in Japan for a company's founders to elect such an early retirement. However, the two men believed that the company would be better managed under more youthful leadership. Fujisawa stated, "It is absolutely essential that a person be named the president of a company during his forties." Once retired, Honda rarely visited the company. "A company prospers when its former head turns up as infrequently as possible," he said.

The company continually strives to maintain the lightness of foot of a small organization, no matter how big it becomes. Managers and associates are reminded that they always must be innovative, that they must live up to the tradition begun by those who paved the way. Even though the company has large reserves to fund major undertakings, employees are told that they must come up with new ideas, and they must act with the same enthusiasm and vigor as their predecessors displayed when funds were limited. "Think about how to use ideas instead of spending money," they are told. Here we have the Honda Motor Company, the world's youngest major automobile company, an organization with a deep and rich sense of culture. And yet the paradox is that the most hated word in the entire organization is *tradition.*

CARRYING THE HONDA TORCH

While it is easier to buy or copy ideas from other companies, Honda refuses to seek technology from outside sources. In the short run, it certainly is more expensive to maintain this kind of independence. But in the long run, the company avoids being put in the undesirable position of having to rely on others for technology that it neither understands nor can develop.

A company that lacks the fundamentals cannot expand existing technology. A quick study of the company's history reveals that since its beginning, Honda has relied on its own technological innovations, never on the ideas of others.

A WINNING SPIRIT

Honda's philosophy is best summed up by its winning spirit, a way of life that demands perfection, however impossible it is to achieve. The status quo is never acceptable.

Honda is committed to making highly efficient products at reasonable prices. In every aspect of its designing, engineering, and manufacturing processes, the company is never satisfied to reach only a reasonable level of efficiency. Each year new models have been developed to what was believed to be the "limit." In each succeeding year, an all-out effort has been exerted to improve the preceding year's effort.

In January 1985, *Car and Driver* listed the Honda Accord among the ten best cars sold in the United States for the third consecutive year. The magazine stated, "There is nothing wrong with a Honda Accord. Nothing." Yet the following September, the company made a full model change of the car. Everything was changed. In 1986, 1987, and 1988, *Car and Driver* again named the Accord as one of its ten best cars in the United States. In 1987, the magazine said:

> The Accord is as close to the universally acceptable automobile as the industry has ever come. . . . It is hard to imagine, but engineers and technicians are doubtlessly planning a new Accord to replace today's model in a couple of years. Short of remodeling the Sistine Chapel or overhauling the Acropolis, we can't conceive of a tougher undertaking.

On March 9, 1988, *Motor Trend,* an authoritative automotive publication, announced the results of the 1988 Import Car of the Year contest, and went on to say:

> For the second time this decade, Honda Motor Company has repeated its heretofore unprecedented 1-2-3 finish . . . The accomplishment is doubly significant, to be sure, as this year's field was

arguably the strongest ever gathered in the history of ICOY [Import Car of the Year].

The article specified that the totally redesigned Honda CRX Si had won the 1988 ICOY, marking the first time in the thirteen-year history of the competition that the same import car manufacturer has claimed consecutive awards. The Civic LX (4-door) sedan and the Prelude Si with four-wheel steering finished second and third in the competition. At Honda, complacency is unthinkable.

There is no doubt that the racing spirit has planted deep seeds within the corporate culture of Honda. A winner-take-all attitude prevails. In its racing activities throughout the world, second place is seldom remembered and never honored. At Honda, winning the race always is the final goal. The company believes it must direct every resource and power to achieve this goal.

Appendix
A Brief History of Honda

1946

OCTOBER   Honda Technical Research Institute established by Soichiro Honda in Hamamatsu, Shizuoka Prefecture, where internal combustion engines and machine tools were developed and produced.

1948

SEPTEMBER   Honda Technical Research Institute incorporated and renamed Honda Motor Company Ltd., capitalized at 1 million yen, or approximately $7,000.

1949

OCTOBER   Takeo Fujisawa, who is considered a cofounder of Honda, joins the company.

1952

JUNE   F-type Cub motorcycle exported to Taiwan.

1954

MARCH   Honda Motor Company Ltd. announces participation in Britain's Isle of Man Tourist Trophy (TT) Race.

1955

SEPTEMBER   Honda Motor Company Ltd. takes the lead in annual domestic motorcycle production.

1959

JUNE   American Honda Motor Company, Inc., established.

1960

APRIL   Suzuka Factory starts operation in Suzuka City, Mie Prefecture.

JULY   Research and development division incorporated as Honda R&D Company Ltd.

1961

MAY   European Honda (now Honda Deutschland) established in Hamburg, West Germany.

OCTOBER   Honda racing team wins the Manufacturers' Championships in the 125-cc and 250-cc classes at the 1961 World Motorcycle Grand Prix.

1962

MARCH   Honda kicked off an advertising campaign that would revolutionize motorcycle history in the United States: "You Meet the Nicest People on A Honda."

SEPTEMBER   N.V. Honda Motor S.A. (now Honda Belgium N.V.) established to assemble and sell mopeds in Europe.
Construction of Suzuka Circuit completed. Honda Koki Engineering established, which was later in-

corporated and renamed Honda Engineering Company Ltd.

DECEMBER   Honda issues ADR (American Depository Receipts) in the United States.

1963

MARCH   Honda issues EDR (European Depository Receipts) in Europe.

MAY   Honda Benelux plant in Belgium starts production of mopeds.

NOVEMBER   Honda racing team wins the Manufacturers' Championships in 250-cc and 350-cc classes at the World Grand Prix Road Race.

1964

JANUARY   Honda Motor Company Ltd. announces participation in F-I car racing.

AUGUST   Honda auto racing team participates in the German F-I Race (1,500-cc class) for the first time.

SEPTEMBER   Honda France S.A. established in Paris.

OCTOBER   Asian Honda Motor Company Ltd. established in Thailand.

NOVEMBER   Automobile production starts at Saitama Factory.

1965

FEBRUARY   Export of S600 started.

SEPTEMBER   Honda (U.K.) Ltd. established in London.

OCTOBER   Honda F-I car wins the Mexico Grand Prix Race (1,500-cc class).

1966

APRIL
Thai Honda Manufacturing Company Ltd. (motorcycle production facility) established in Bangkok, Thailand.

SEPTEMBER
Honda racing team wins the Manufacturers' Championships in 50-cc, 125-cc, 250-cc, 350-cc, and 500-cc classes in the World Motorcycle Championship Grand Prix race—the first time a manufacturer won 5 classes.
Honda F-2 car establishes a world record of eleven consecutive victories.

1967

SEPTEMBER
Honda F-1 wins Italian Grand Prix Race (3,000-cc class).

OCTOBER
Production of automobiles started at Suzuka Factory.

1969

MARCH
Canadian Honda Motor Ltd. (now Honda Canada, Inc.) established in Toronto, Canada.

APRIL
Dream CB750 Four exported to the United States and Canada.

1970

MARCH
Honda N600 exported to the United States. The little car got an impressive 42 miles per gallon in city driving.
First All Honda Idea Contest held at Suzuka Circuit.

1971

FEBRUARY   Honda CVCC (Compound Vortex Controlled Combustion) engine announced, world's first to comply with 1970 Statutory Clean Air Act in the United States.

JUNE   Motorcycle production starts in Mexico.

NOVEMBER   Honda Motor do Brasil Ltd. established in Sao Paulo, Brazil.

1972

SEPTEMBER   Honda International Trading Corporation, a subsidiary of American Honda Motor Company, Inc., established.

1973

JULY   CVCC license agreement signed with Ford Motor Company.

OCTOBER   President Soichiro Honda and Executive Vice-President Takeo Fujisawa retire and become supreme advisers.
Kiyoshi Kawashima becomes president.

NOVEMBER   Civic Hatchback awarded the 1974 Import Car-of-the-Year Prize by *Road Test* magazine, United States.

DECEMBER   Act Maritime Corporation established (Operation of Car Carriers).

1974

MAY   The CVCC engine development group awarded the 1973 Society's Prize by the Society of Automotive Engineers.

JULY   Honda Engineering Company Ltd. established. Honda del Peru S.A. established in Lima, Peru. Honda International Sales Company (HISCO) signs a contract with Ford Japan for sales of Ford products in Japan.

OCTOBER   Production of mini-compact cars curtailed.

NOVEMBER   Civic CVCC passes the exhaust emission test given by the Environmental Protection Agency (EPA).

1975

MARCH   Civic awarded the Economy Prize by *Motor Trend* magazine, United States.

JUNE   Patent right for general ideas of CVCC engine system approved and later announced in the United States (25 patents approved by the end of June).

JULY   Moto Honda da Amazonia Limitada established in Brazil.

1976

APRIL   The first Accord (hatchback model) was named *Motor Trend* magazine's "Import Car of the Year."

1977

JANUARY   Motorcycle Production begins at Motor Honda da Amazonia Limitada in Manaus, Brazil.

MARCH   Civic CVCC ranked first place in Fuel Economy Test for 1977 models by EPA and FEA (Federal Energy Association) of the United States.

JUNE   Consolidated financial statement issued for the first time in the Japanese automotive industry.

OCTOBER   Plans to establish a $35 million motorcycle plant in Marysville, Ohio, announced.

1978

MARCH   Honda of America Manufacturing, Inc. (HAM), established as a joint venture of Honda Motor Company Ltd. and American Honda Motor Company, Inc.; assumes charge of motorcycle production in Ohio.

APRIL   Honda Europe N.V. established in Ghent, Belgium, as a part of program to improve the local procurement and distribution system.

1979

SEPTEMBER   Honda of America Manufacturing, Inc., starts motorcycle production. Honda made a second major announcement: An automobile production facility would be built adjacent to the motorcycle plant. The sporty Prelude and the four-door Accord were introduced.

DECEMBER   Honda signs a technical collaboration agreement with BL Limited, under which BL will produce a new car designed by Honda.

1980

JANUARY   The Civic 1500 second generation introduced.

APRIL   Honda Motor Company Ltd. becomes the first Japanese manufacturer among those established after World War II to achieve annual unconsolidated net sales in excess of 1 trillion yen.

1981

JUNE BL Limited begins producing Triumph Acclaim cars under license with Honda.

OCTOBER BL Limited launches Triumph Acclaim cars under license with Honda.

NOVEMBER Announcement that Honda Motor Company Ltd. and BL Limited will jointly develop and manufacture a "luxury" car.

1982

JANUARY The second generation Accord is introduced.

APRIL Honda of America produces its 100,000th motorcycle.

NOVEMBER Honda of America begins car production with the Accord.

1983

APRIL The second-generation Prelude is introduced.

JULY Spirit-Honda F-1 makes its debut at Silverstone Circuit, England.

AUGUST Honda Power Equipment Manufacturing, Inc., established in North Carolina.

OCTOBER Kiyoshi Kawashima retires as president and becomes supreme adviser.
Tadashi Kume becomes president.

1984

JANUARY Plans announced to double car production capacity to 300,000 units per year at Honda of America Manufacturing, Inc.

The Civic CRX and third-generation Civic Wagon and Hatchback are new introductions.

FEBRUARY   *Motor Trend* magazine named Civic CRX as the "1984 Import Car of the Year." For the first time, one company takes the first, second, and third places: CRX followed by Prelude and Civic Hatchback.

MARCH   Honda selects Anna, Ohio, for its $40 million motorcycle engine plant site.

APRIL   Honda Motor and Austin Rover Group (former BL Ltd.) sign a manufacturing agreement on the luxury project.

JUNE   Plans announced to establish an automobile plant in Ontario, Canada.
Ceremony marking the twenty-fifth anniversary of American Honda Motor Company, Inc., is held.
Honda Power Equipment Manufacturing, Inc., starts production of lawn mowers.
American Honda announced it would create a new auto division—Acura—in 1986 that would sell a new line of performance luxury cars.

SEPTEMBER   Honda Research of America established (now Honda R&D North America, Inc.).

OCTOBER   American Honda Motor Company, Inc., establishes American Honda Foundation.

1985

JANUARY   *Car and Driver* magazine selects the Accord as one of its ten best cars of the year.

MARCH   Plans announced to establish a power products plant in France.

MAY   Honda Engineering Company Ltd. opens U.S. branch in Ohio.

JUNE   Canadian Acura sales network announced.
Honda announces plan for production of automobile engine in United States.
Honda signs a collaborative memorandum with BL to increase joint activities, including development of new compact cars.

DECEMBER   Plans announced to double car production capacity in Canada from 40,000 to 80,000 units.

1986

FEBRUARY   Honda begins power product production in France.
Honda unveiled a completely restyled and retooled third-generation Accord four-door. It was named to *Motor Trend*'s list of the ten best imported cars.

MARCH   Acura sales network in United States begins sales of Legend and Integra.

APRIL   Honda Motor and Austin Rover Group sign an agreement, under which ARG will produce Honda Ballade.
Honda of America begins car production on second assembly line.

MAY   Plans announced to use Central Gulf Lines, Inc., United States, for shipment of cars.

JULY   The first Civic built in the United States rolled off the second line at the Marysville, Ohio, assembly plant.

AUGUST   Honda rated number one in 1986 U.S. Customer Satisfaction Index by J. D. Power.

SEPTEMBER   Honda captures 1986 F-1 Constructors' Championship.

Honda of America Manufacturing, Inc., begins engine production in Anna, Ohio.

The first 1.5-liter Civic engine was produced at the Anna, Ohio, engine facility.

OCTOBER   Honda develops world's first steer-angle-dependent four-wheel steering system (4WS).

NOVEMBER   Honda of Canada begins producing Accord in Alliston, Ontario.

DECEMBER   Honda Motor and Austin Rover Group sign an agreement for joint design and development of a new medium car code-named YY.

Car and Driver names Honda Accord as one of 1986's "10 Best Cars of the Year" in the United States domestic division, as well as the Acura Integra in the import car division.

1987

JANUARY   An additional investment of $450 million in the Anna, Ohio, engine plant is announced.

MARCH   Acura Legend Coupe introduced.

AUGUST   J. D. Power Customer Satisfaction Index rates Acura and Honda first and second, respectively.

SEPTEMBER   Five-part strategy for North America announced. The plan includes: a second U.S. auto plant in Ohio; expansion of engine plant; exports of American-made cars and motorcycles to Japan and other world markets; increase of local content to 75 percent; expansion of R&D and engineering staffs in the United States.

Fourth-generation Civic introduced.

Third-generation Prelude introduced with four-wheel steering as option.

NOVEMBER   Honda captures 1987 F-1 Constructor's Championship

Chapter Notes

Page   CHAPTER 1

4. "Art Shokai": Sol Sanders, *Honda: The Man and the Machines* (Boston: Little Brown and Company, 1975) pp. 22–25.

5. "Repairing cars is limited": Sanders; p. 43.

5. "No matter how hard you labor": Sanders, p. 45.

5. "Hamamatsu School of Technology": Sanders, p. 46.

5. "A ticket will get you a seat": Sanders, p. 47.

5. "Japanese *gakubatsu*": Sanders, p. 48.

6. "Takeo Fujisawa": Tetsuo Sakiya, *Honda Motor: The Men, the Management, the Machines* (Tokyo and New York: Kodansha International USA Ltd., 1982), pp. 42–45.

8. "In a twist of fate": Sakiya, pp. 64–66.

8. "All of the local investors": Sakiya, p. 65.

9. "Assuming that reaching the top of Mount Fuji": Sakiya, p. 66.

9. "Monthly production again zoomed: "Honda," *Harvard Business School Review,* 1983, pp. 1–2.

10. "We no longer will sell only our engines": "Honda," p. 2.

11. "*Zaibatsu*": Tetsuo Sakiya, *Honda Motor: The Men, the Management, the Machines* (Tokyo and New York: Kodansha International USA Ltd., 1982), p. 58.

13. "Most Japanese employees are urged": Susan Chira, "At 80, Honda's Founder Is Still a Fiery Maverick," *New York Times,* January 2, 1987.

14. "Called Kaminari-san—'Mr. Thunder'—": Chira.

16. "By the time Honda Motor Company participated": George Gilder, *The Spirit of Enterprise* (New York: Simon & Schuster, 1984), p. 190.

17. "In 1958, Honda introduced the 50-cc Supercub": Tetsuo Sakiya, *Honda Motor: The Men, the Management, the Machines* (Tokyo and New York: Kodansha International USA Ltd., 1982), p. 118.

19. "Government officials should always act to protect": Chira.

20. "A new world that now includes a formidable rival, Japan": Lee Iacocca with William Novak, *Iacocca* (New York: Bantam Books, 1985), p. 207.

20. "The field where this game is being played is not level.": Iacocca, p. 315.

23. "Air-cooling is the limit of my experience": Tetsuo Sakiya, *Honda Motor: The Men, the Management, the Machines* (Tokyo and New York: Kodansha International USA Ltd., 1982) p. 160.

Page

CHAPTER 2

25. "Face the toughest challenges first": Elliot Borin, "Enter Honda," *Motorcyclist,* July 1987, pp. 73–75.

26. "Its population density of 318 people per km": *Passport to Japan* (Tokyo: Business Intercommunications, Inc., 1984), p. 3.

27. "By the early 1600s": Robert C. Christopher, *The Japanese Mind* (New York: Linden Press/Simon & Schuster, 1983), p. 185.

27. "Americans who cling to our national heritage": Turney, p. 83.

29. "During the course of the conversation": Elliot Borin, "Enter Honda," *Motorcyclist,* July 1987, p. 76.

32. "In the United States its sales force contacted all conceivable retailers": Borin, p. 79.

34. "You Meet the Nicest People": Tetsuo Sakiya, *Honda Motor: The Men, the Management, the Machines* (Tokyo and New York: Kodansha International USA Ltd., 1982), pp. 124–125.

CHAPTER 4

59. "Offbeat motorcycle ads have become a trademark": Ronald Alsop, "Can Honda Scooter Ads Get Any More Offbeat Than This?" *Wall Street Journal,* June 4, 1987, p. 27.

60. "Late in 1972 Honda shipped three cars": Albert Q. Maisel, "From Japan— A 'Clean' Car that Saves Gas," *Reader's Digest,* December 1975, pp. 103–104.

63. "The Voluntary Restraint Agreement that Japan adopted in 1981": Joan Berger, "Will the Auto Glut Choke Detroit?" *Business Week,* March 7, 1988, p. 60.

66. "When we [Honda] introduced the second generation Prelude": Jerry Flint, "Nobody Likes Us Except the Consumer," *Forbes,* October 19, 1987, p. 56.

67. "In November 1987, Volkswagen became the first": Joseph R. White and Thomas P. O'Boyle, "Volkswagen AG to Close or Sell Its U.S. Plant," *Wall Street Journal,* November 23, 1987, pp. 2, 15.

68. "According to a 1985 Gallup survey": *Consumer Perceptions Concerning the Quality of American Products and Services* (a study by the Gallup Organization for the American Society for Quality Control, 1985), pp. 12–13.

69. "With a perfect reading":*Road and Track,* November 1987.

69. "It is too early to pronounce the Acura": John Holusha, "In U.S., New Cars Court the Affluent," *New York Times,* June 15, 1987.

69. "Honda has risen to its currently lofty status": Greg Brown, "Acura Legend, a Propitious Debut for Honda's Luxury Sedan," *Motor Trend,* March 1987, p. 72.

69. "A trendsetter in the U.S. market": Christopher A. Amatos, "Honda Stays with Winning Formula," *Columbus Dispatch,* September 20, 1987, p. 5H.

70. "Honda feared some luxury-car buyers": Haya El Nasser, "Honda Makes It Less Simple," *USA Today,* March 28, 1986, p. 1B.

70. "A demographics study shows these buyers are well-educated": John Holusha, "In U.S. New Cars Court the Affluent," *New York Times,* June 15, 1987.

CHAPTER 5

76. "Watson said that he wanted IBM": Buck Rodgers with Robert L. Shook, *The IBM Way* (New York: Harper & Row Publishers, 1986), p. 16.

78. "Service can't be an afterthought": Rodgers, p. 167.

Page

78. "Frequently carries a steep up-front cost": Karen Pennar, "The Push for Quality," *Business Week,* June 8, 1987, p. 136.

80. "Consumers increasingly find themselves paying more for service": Joan Berger, "In the Service Sector—Nothing Is 'Free' Anymore," *Business Week,* June 8, 1987, p. 144.

80. "Who would have thought": Tom Peters, *Thriving on Chaos* (New York: Alfred A. Knopf, 1987), p. 59.

83. "It's a shame": Robert L. Shook, *Ten Greatest Salespersons* (New York: Harper & Row Publishers, 1978), p. 68.

83. "A successful real estate salesperson": Shook, p. 104.

83. "Customers have the perception that service": Stanley Marcus, *Quest for the Best* (New York: The Viking Press, 1979), p. 44.

85. "It's a day-in, day-out, ongoing": Bro Uttal, "Companies That Serve You Best," *Fortune,* December 7, 1987, p. 98.

CHAPTER 6

96. "If juniors don't rebel against their seniors": Susan Chira, *New York Times,* June 15, 1987, business section, page 1.

96. "One thing I never say is": Tetsuo Sakiya, *Honda Motor: The Men, the Management, the Machines* (Tokyo and New York: Kodansha International USA Ltd., 1982), p. 189.

CHAPTER 12

166. "You have to act as if everyone around you is a guest": Susan Chira, "At 80, Honda's Founder Is Still a Fiery Maverick," *Wall Street Journal,* January 2, 1987.

167. "There are also mock production lines": Richard Koenig, "Toyota Takes Pains, Time, Filling Jobs at Its Kentucky Plant," *Wall Street Journal,* December 1, 1987, p. 21.

168. "At its Smyrna, Tennessee plant, Nissan": Koenig, p. 21.

CHAPTER 13

183. "We Japanese feel that all things are provided as a sacred trust": Akio Morita, *Made in Japan* (New York: E. P. Dutton, 1986), p. 227.

183. "We Japanese are obsessed with survival": Morita, p. 226.

183. "The average Japanese puts about 20 percent": Robert C. Christopher, *The Japanese Mind* (New York: Linden Press/Simon & Schuster, New York, 1983), p. 272.

184. "While Europe and America discontinued energy projects": Stephen Kreider Yoder, "Japan Persists in Costly Energy Research," *Wall Street Journal,* June 2, 1987, p. 26.

184. "It shows how much of a crisis mentality": Yoder, p. 26.

184. "Some are saying we should slow down": Yoder, p. 26.

185. "Japanese companies can afford to wait": Stephen Kreider Yoder, "Japan's Troubled Industries Stress R&D," *Wall Street Journal,* March 25, 1987, p. 24.

185. "Unlike stockholders, bankers do not stand to gain directly": Robert C. Christopher, *The Japanese Mind* (New York: Linden Press/Simon & Schuster, 1983), p. 254.

185. "Kawasaki Steel": Stephen Kreider Yoder, "Japan's Troubled Industries Stress R&D," *Wall Street Journal,* March 25, 1987, p. 24.

Page

186. "Bethlehem Steel Corporation cut its research": Yoder, p. 24.

186. "We have to bite the bullet today": Yoder, p. 24.

186. "If we don't do our R&D now": Yoder, p. 24.

186. "When things get tough": Yoder, p. 24.

188. "To establish Honda in America as an American corporation": *Barron's Weekly,* December 1, 1985.

189. "Soichiro Honda, himself, produced more than 470 patented ideas": Susan Chira, "At 80, Honda's Founder Is Still a Fiery Maverick," *New York Times,* January 2, 1987.

CHAPTER 14

196. "In Japan, there are approximately 17,000 lawyers": Akio Morita, *Made in Japan* (New York: E. P. Dutton, 1986), pp. 173–174.

199. "Big, not best, has always been the American calling card": Tom Peters, *Thriving on Chaos* (New York: Alfred A. Knopf, 1987), p. 13.

200. "Listen to the chatter when the Fortune 500 comes out": Peters, p. 4.

200. "If you can't point to something specific": Peters, p. 464.

202. "Barely 800 U.S. citizens are studying at Japanese universities": Joel Dreyfuss, "How Japan Picks America's Brains," *Fortune,* December 21, 1987, p. 84.

CHAPTER 15

208. "For any organization to survive and achieve success": Buck Rodgers, *The IBM Way* (New York: Harper & Row, 1986), p. 18.

209. "G.E.: 'Progress is our most important product' ": Terrance E. Deal and Allan A. Kennedy, *Corporate Cultures* (Reading, Massachusetts: Addison-Wesley Publishing Company, 1982), p. 6.

209. "Sears, Roebuck: 'Quality at a good price": Deal and Kennedy, p. 23.

214. "It is absolutely essential": Tetsuo Sakiya, *Honda Motor: The Men, the Management, the Machines* (Tokyo and New York: Kodansha International USA Ltd., 1982) p. 182.

214. "A company prospers when its former head": Lloyd Garrison, *Time* (International Edition), September 8, 1986, p. 000.

215. "There is nothing wrong with the Honda Accord. Nothing": *Car and Driver,* January 1985.

215. "The Accord is as close to the universally acceptable automobile": *Car and Driver,* 1987.

215. "For the second time this decade": "1988 Import Car of the Year," *Motor Trend,* April 1988, p. 138.

Index